EAST CENTRAL EUROPE FROM REFORM TO TRANSFORMATION

Judy Batt

PUBLISHED IN NORTH AMERICA FOR

THE ROYAL INSTITUTE OF INTERNATIONAL AFFAIRS

COUNCIL ON FOREIGN RELATIONS PRESS
• NEW YORK •

Chatham House Papers

A Soviet Foreign Policy Programme Publication
Programme Director: Neil Malcolm

The Royal Institute of International Affairs, at Chatham House in London, has provided an impartial forum for discussion and debate on current international issues for 70 years. Its resident research fellows, specialized information resources, and range of publications, conferences, and meetings span the fields of international politics, economics, and security. The Institute is independent of government.

Chatham House Papers are short monographs on current policy problems which have been commissioned by the RIIA. In preparing the papers, authors are advised by a study group of experts convened by the RIIA, and publication of a paper indicates that the Institute regards it as an authoritative contribution to the public debate. The Institute does not, however, hold opinions of its own; the views expressed in this publication are the responsibility of the author.

Library of Congress Cataloguing-in-Publication Data

Batt, Judy.
  East Central Europe : from reform to transformation / by Judy Batt.
      p.   cm.—(Chatham House papers)
  Originally published: London : Pinter, 1991.
  Includes bibliographical references.
  ISBN 0-87609-106-0 : $14.95
1. Poland—Economic policy—1981– 2. Poland—Politics and government—1989– 3. Hungary—Economic policy—1989– 4. Hungary—Politics and government—1989– 5. Czechoslovakia—Economic Policy—1965– 6. Czechoslovakia—Politics and government—1989–
I. Title II. Series: Chatham House papers (Unnumbered)
HC340.3.B385 1991
338.943—dc20   91-19513
                                                             CIP

91 92 93 94 95 96 97 PB 10 9 8 7 6 5 4 3 2 1

CONTENTS

ACKNOWLEDGMENTS

Much of the preparatory work for this paper was done during the year I spent with the Royal Institute of International Affairs, at Chatham House, January-December 1990, working on a collaborative project on Comparative Reforms in Socialist Countries, supported financially by the Sasakawa Peace Foundation. Chapters 1 and 2 draw heavily on a paper written for this project and presented at a workshop on Comparative Socialist Reforms, which was held at the Woodrow Wilson Center, Washington DC, in October 1990. I am especially grateful to Neil Malcolm, Head of the Soviet Programme at Chatham House, for suggesting that I develop the original workshop paper into a Chatham House Paper, and for his encouragement and support while I carried out the work. I received much useful advice from the Chatham House editorial staff, Pauline Wickham and Hannah Doe. Drafts of the paper were discussed at two study groups at Chatham House in December 1990 and February 1991, which contributed much to the shape and factual accuracy of the final version. I would like to thank the participants in those study groups, and, in particular, George Schöpflin and Bill Lomax, who made many detailed comments. Susan O'Reilly and Max Rutherstone kindly provided me with accommodation and excellent hospitality in London while I worked at Chatham House, and, last but not least, Martin Cherry provided the companionship, moral support and good home cooking which sustained me during particularly intensive bouts of work on the manuscript.

April 1991   Judy Batt

INTRODUCTION

This book deals with three countries of East Central Europe, Poland, Hungary and Czechoslovakia, which have much in common as a result of their geographical location, level of socio-economic development and recent political history. To that extent, it makes sense to treat them together, and it makes possible fruitful comparisons that serve to highlight not only the similarities but also the important differences in the patterns of their politics and economics in the transition from Soviet-style state socialism. The other countries of Eastern Europe, Bulgaria, Romania and Yugoslavia, share to some extent the problems of the three 'Northern Tier' countries covered in this book, but they also have many historical, cultural and other peculiarities which warrant separate treatment, and which are dealt with by Christopher Cviic in his Chatham House Paper, *Remaking the Balkans* (1991).

The focus of this study is on the interaction between politics and economics. Chapter 1 deals with the political impact of failed reform on communist rule in each country. In Poland and Hungary, the communist leaderships made repeated, but inconsistent and unsuccessful, attempts at economic reform. The cumulation of these failures resulted not only in deepening economic difficulties but in the political exhaustion of the regimes themselves. In Czechoslovakia, by contrast, the Husak regime, installed in the wake of the 1968 Warsaw Pact invasion of the country, remained militantly committed to the end to the traditional tenets of Marxist-Leninist ideology, and to the bureaucratic-centralist pattern of economic management modelled on the Soviet system under Brezhnev. The arrival of Mikhail Gorbachev on the Soviet political scene obviously

1

had an enormous impact on each of these countries, and this is discussed in Chapter 2. In none of the three countries had the communist regimes managed to build up more than the narrowest domestic political base, and, as it became clear that Moscow had abandoned the 'Brezhnev Doctrine', the demise of these regimes was inevitable. But, as Chapter 2 outlines, each went its own way.

With the demise of communist rule, a plethora of new movements and parties has sprung up. Chapter 3 looks into the cultural and historical background from which new political groupings can be expected to emerge. Although many of the first parties to spring to life were revivals of parties that had existed in the pre-communist period, in fact the wholly new political movements that came into being have been the most successful in gathering members and in winning elections. But they have rapidly run into problems connected with their initial aversion to formalized party organization and the incompatibility of their original form as broad, anti-communist coalitions and the new tasks of policy-making and implementation in government.

In Chapter 4, we return to the theme of political-economic interaction, now in the context of economic transformation. The contrast between the tasks of 'reform' and 'transformation' is spelt out in the first section of the chapter. The central point of contrast is identified in the role of private property. Socialist economic reforms assumed it was possible to resurrect an efficient market economy without restoring private ownership. The conclusion drawn by most of Eastern Europe's economists from the bitter experience of the past decades is that the two are inseparable. An important element in the politics of economic transformation is thus the question of privatization. But, as the second section of the chapter seeks to show, this should be seen in the general context of the formation of 'strong' governments in East Central Europe: that is, governments that are capable not only of addressing the issues and formulating appropriate policies, but of sustaining political and social support through the inevitably traumatic and disorienting period of transition from a state-socialist to a liberal-capitalist economy. It is too early to pass judgment on the record of the governments of East Central Europe in this respect. What the final section of Chapter 4 attempts to do is simply to present an account of the problems encountered to date.

An Appendix, including summaries of the electoral system in each country and the results of recent elections, has been added, to which readers should refer for more detailed information than could be included in the main text.

1

ECONOMIC REFORM IN THE CRISIS OF COMMUNIST RULE

Communist rule in Eastern Europe owed its origins in the late 1940s to three conditions: the external force of the Soviet Union, which dominated the region at the end of the Second World War; the readiness of a determined minority of communists in each country to use coercion, deception and manipulation of their fellow countrymen in order to secure a monopoly of power for the Communist Party; and the physical exhaustion and political disorientation of the war-ravaged populations.[1] Communist rule broke down in 1989 because it had proved quite unable to remove the stigma of its coercive origins and to live up to the ambitious promises of economic modernization, material welfare and social justice that are contained in the ideology of Marxism-Leninism and that justify the Communist Party's monopoly of power. By 1989, the three original conditions of communist rule in Eastern Europe had changed completely. The leadership of the Soviet Communist Party now recognized that the economic and political costs of preserving Soviet control over Eastern Europe were no longer sustainable. Key groups within the East European communist elites were demoralized by the manifest failures of their period of rule and showed clear signs of losing the sense of purpose and discipline that the ideology had provided. Meanwhile, the populations of Eastern Europe had developed over the past four decades from impoverished and intimidated masses into relatively well-educated people, who were, moreover, increasingly well informed about the world beyond the confines of 'real socialism' and increasingly frustrated by their economic and political lot.

In this chapter, we will trace the trajectories of the communist regimes

3

of Poland, Hungary and Czechoslovakia towards their final demise. Although, as suggested above, there were common basic factors in the breakdown of communist rule throughout Eastern Europe, there were also significant differences in the way in which these factors worked themselves out in each case. After Stalin's death, the uniformity of the political and economic systems of the East European satellites gave way to increasing diversity as the communist regimes struggled to stabilize their power by supplementing the crude coercion of the Stalin period with some concessions to 'national specifics', to economic incentives, and to the provision of an acceptable level of material welfare for the population. From the late 1950s, the issue of economic reform came to occupy centre-stage in the East European political arena, but with varying economic and political results. In the analysis that follows, the problem of economic reform is identified as fundamental to the breakdown of communist rule in the three countries. In Poland and Hungary, the regimes embarked on reform as a means of shoring up communist power, but the half-way reforms that they introduced turned out to be worse than no reform at all, while radical reform (that is, reform that would bring about the intended economic results) would have undermined communist power. The Czechoslovak communists after 1968 were fully aware of this logic and so pursued a different path of intransigent resistance to reform, reverting to the Stalinist patterns of coercion, doctrinaire ideology and a high degree of dependence on the Soviet Union in order to stabilize their rule. They preserved the illusion of economic stability, but this was increasingly unconvincing to the Czechoslovak population, who saw no improvement in their standard of living in the 1980s. The Czechoslovak communist regime was thus in an exceptionally weak position to confront the challenge posed from outside by Gorbachev's policy of *perestroika*, and eventually collapsed even more rapidly than the Polish and Hungarian regimes.

Although the end-result was the same in each case, it is nevertheless worth looking more closely at the different patterns of breakdown, because these have significant implications for the subsequent phases of the transition, as will become clear in the following chapters.

The path of failed reform in Poland and Hungary
Economic reform was the central plank of the political strategy of the Polish and Hungarian communist regimes. It was an attempt to stabilize power after traumatic political crises which had exposed unambiguously

the essentially coercive basis of the party's power and its role as the instrument of national subordination to the Soviet Union. The regimes evidently expected that reform would inject new life into the communist ideology and would revive the legitimacy of the political system by demonstrating the party's efficacy as the agent of economic and social modernization and the provider of levels of personal consumption and social welfare comparable with, if not superior to, those of the West. They also promised that economic reform would open up new opportunities for promotion and high material reward for the ambitious, well-qualified and hard-working.

In fact, economic reform was adopted as a form of substitute politics: purposes that are properly those of politics were thrust onto the economy. Participation, the expression, competition and reconciliation of interests, and the enjoyment of a sphere of individual freedom were all to be realized in the economic sphere by, for example, increasing the independence of enterprises from central interference, offering performance-related material incentives, and relaxing the restrictions on private economic activity. The sphere of politics, however, remained monopolized by the communist party as before. The leadership seems to have expected that replacing command-planning by the regulated market would, in effect, transform the basis of party rule from coercion to consent, and that economic efficiency would translate into moral legitimacy.

The structure of power that evolved as a result of the adoption of the reformist strategy in Hungary and Poland in the late 1960s and early 1970s can be described as a form of 'state corporatism'[2] or 'consultative authoritarianism',[3] in which the eventual crisis and breakdown were already prefigured. Alongside the partial decentralization of control over the economy, the strict centralization of political power through the communist party's disciplined hierarchy gave way to a diffusion of power among regional party apparatuses, sectoral ministries and large, industrial conglomerates, all of which began to act as powerful lobbies in central decision-making. In particular, they were heavily represented on the Central Committee, the key body of the communist party, which had ultimately the power to accept or reject major policy changes and to change the party leadership. The central party leadership and government thus became highly responsive to these bureaucratic interests, if not dependent on them.[4]

At first sight, this could be taken as evidence of political development, in the sense of evolution in the direction of a more pluralistic and rational politics based on more open expression and competition of interests.[5] In

5

fact, it was a highly imperfect, unregulated form of political decentralization, which transmitted social interests in a selective, distorted way, and
which seriously weakened the ability of the central authorities to construct and implement coherent policies, and, in particular, to maintain
overall macroeconomic control.[6] In Hungary, this weakness became
apparent with the compromises and modifications to the New Economic
Mechanism between 1972 and 1975, which amounted to a major reversal
of the reform; while in Poland, in the second half of the 1970s, Edvard
Gierek found himself unable to impose the necessary policies of economic adjustment, and thus he was unable to prevent the economy from
sliding into crisis in 1980.

The logic of market-type reform was undermined by the traditional,
bureaucratic structure of industrial organization, which remained in being despite the introduction of economic reforms, and in which powerful
conservative interests were entrenched. Thus the industrial branch ministries, which had supervisory powers over enterprises and, in particular,
had the power to appoint and promote enterprise managers, were left in
place despite being in principle superfluous once traditional directive
planning had been abolished and enterprises were supposed to respond to
market signals. Those organizational reforms that took place not only
failed to break up the economically (and often also technologically)
unjustified large industrial enterprises, but even promoted further
mergers and concentration. A significant proportion of enterprises thus
enjoyed monopoly positions on the domestic market, and, because the
governments adopted protectionist economic policies in response to the
developments in the world economy in the 1970s, these enterprises were
not exposed to the rigours of competition from imports either. They were
powerfully placed to evade or manipulate central price and wage regulations, and to secure privileged access to investment resources and
budgetary subsidies.[7]

In both countries, wage payments ran ahead of output and productivity growth. In the Polish case, this was a result of the Gierek regime's
deliberately expansionist incomes policy in the early 1970s and its
powerlessness in the face of mass working-class pressure in the late
1970s.[8] In Hungary, the official trade unions built themselves up as an
effective lobby of self-appointed defenders of the workers' interests.
They derived considerable political clout on policy-making bodies by
acting in concert with the lobby of large enterprises, and by playing on
the party leadership's fears of Polish-style social unrest.[9]

Sustaining the momentum of this pattern of political economy entailed a sharp rise in external indebtedness in both countries, but the expected improvements in export performance on which the strategy depended did not materialize. The governments could blame this on the Western recession, but economic experts recognized that the underlying reason was the failure to improve the quality and technological level of products, because the economic reforms themselves had been inadequate and had not provided sufficient pressures and incentives to force enterprises to change their patterns of behaviour. The problem was compounded by the adoption in both countries of protectionist economic policies that maintained the separation of domestic production from the world market. Both governments, moreover, remained committed to achieving high levels of growth virtually regardless of cost, which further intensified the problems. And so, at the end of a decade of what had amounted to a 'second industrialization', accompanied by much modernizing and reformist rhetoric, Hungary and Poland faced the 1980s with massive, unmanageable hard-currency debts, inefficient and outdated production structures, budget deficits and powerful inflationary pressures.

It is from this time that we can date the beginning of the breakdown of the political system in these two countries. This was, of course, patently obvious in Poland in 1980–81, with the emergence of Solidarity, the unofficial trade union, and the collapse of the Polish United Workers' Party (PUWP), followed by the imposition of martial law. But in Hungary, too, the turn of the decade saw the beginning of a process of gradual, rather more subtle but no less inexorable, erosion of the rule of the Hungarian Socialist Workers' Party (HSWP). Both regimes had come to recognize that further – more radical and consistent – economic reforms were an unavoidable component of any programme for economic recovery, but economic reform by now had become far more risky from the point of view of preserving the communist parties' political power than had been the case in previous reform attempts. Economic reform in the 1980s was to be introduced in conditions of profound economic difficulty in Hungary and open crisis in Poland. Now, therefore, it had to be accompanied by harsh economic policies that in Hungary would at best mean stagnation in the standard of living, and in Poland would entail swingeing price rises and a sharp fall in real wages. In such an environment, economic reform could no longer substitute for political reform – in fact, economic reform now would not be possible without political reform. But political reform itself appeared to be impossible in the declining years of Brezhnev's leadership in Moscow.

The beginning of the final denouement in Hungary can be traced back to a series of plenary sessions of the HSWP Central Committee in October 1977 and during 1978 at which it was acknowledged that the economic policies of the 1970s had been mistaken, and, in particular, that the reversal of the economic reform had contributed in large part to the looming threat of national insolvency.[10] From the summer of 1979, a 'stabilization programme' was introduced, which involved austerity measures to cut investment in order to improve the convertible-currency trade balance while protecting social consumption. The economic reform was relaunched with a price reform designed to bring domestic prices closer to world prices. A series of new measures introduced in the early 1980s not only returned to the original principles of the 1968 New Economic Mechanism, but in certain respects extended and went beyond them. Even so, they were to prove both too little and too late. The industrial branch ministries were merged into a single Ministry of Industry in 1980; many of the large enterprises were broken up into smaller, more viable and competitive, units; the establishment of new small and medium-sized firms was promoted; and new legislation increased the scope for private enterprises and cooperatives. In 1984–5, worker self-management and elected enterprise councils were introduced, transferring from the branch ministries to enterprises the right to control major managerial decisions and to select the top managerial personnel. Liberalization of foreign trade took place with the reduction of the role of the Ministry of Foreign Trade (which was merged with the Ministry of Internal Trade in December 1987), the extension of foreign trade rights to state enterprises, and legislation for joint ventures with Western firms.

In Poland after the introduction of martial law, General Wojciech Jaruzelski reaffirmed the commitment of the regime of 'National Salvation' to the economic reforms that had been prepared in 1980–81. In fact, Jaruzelski and his advisers looked to Kadarist Hungary as a model of social pacification through economic reform.[11] In 1982, the '3-S' programme of 'self-direction, self-financing and self-management' was introduced.[12] Obligatory central plan targets were abolished except for a few strategic industries (for example in coal-mining, the key source of hard-currency exports). Changes were made in the sphere of foreign economic relations, including the extension of foreign trade rights to a larger number of enterprises, and the introduction of new legislation to permit the founding of small foreign firms and, later, joint ventures with foreign capital.

In the conditions of profound economic disequilibrium and pervasive shortages that marked the early period of Jaruzelski's rule, the reforms could be only partially implemented: enterprise autonomy, for example, was crucially vitiated by centralized control over access to most key inputs. Economic recovery in the mid-1980s was weak, and a familiar pattern of political economy quite soon re-established itself: monopolistic producers and industrial lobbies reasserted themselves, and enterprise managers made inflationary wage settlements in order to prevent the eruption of labour unrest and the revival of mass support for Solidarity. Levels of consumption were once again allowed to run ahead of economic performance, thus eroding what had been achieved by the drastic austerity measures of 1982. Convertible-currency trade had begun to show a surplus, but no significant reduction in the huge accumulated debt was possible. Indeed, to maintain even modest growth, further borrowing seemed inevitable. Thus by 1987 it was recognized that the main objectives of the reform had not been achieved, and a renewed, more radical, proposal for a 'Second Stage' of reform as a follow-up to the 1982 measures was unveiled.

In Hungary, a not dissimilar pattern could be discerned. As one Western commentator observed: 'Despite these reform measures, one senses a reluctance to pursue reform as vigorously as in the past as well as a suspicion that reforms increasingly appear to deal with issues peripheral to Hungary's fundamental economic problems and are more style than substance.'[13] The government, over-optimistic after weathering an acute liquidity crisis in 1981–2, and seeing signs of economic recovery in 1983–4, attempted to accelerate the growth rate in 1985. But the underlying weakness of the economy was rapidly exposed by the result: the country's convertible-currency debt doubled between 1985 and 1987, from (gross) $8.8bn to $17.7bn.[14] The stage seemed set for a repeat performance of the Polish crisis of 1980–81.

Political disintegration was both cause and consequence of these economic developments. The diffusion of power had weakened central control over the economy, as well as over the managerial and administrative elites. Corruption became more extensive and more open. Leadership immobilism and drift set in in the face of the intractable politico-economic conundrum: given the framework of the traditional political structure, the reformist leaderships remained prisoners of conservative bureaucratic interests embedded in the party-state hierarchy over which they presided.[15] The implementation of economic reform clearly required political reform in order to mobilize new sources of social support outside this political *apparat*; but political reform was blocked by the seemingly immovable external obstacle of the Brezhnev regime, by the lack of popular credibility of the regimes as a result of their past performance, and by the inertia of profoundly sceptical, pessimistic and politically alienated populations.

Jaruzelski's programme of 'socialist renewal' involved an attempt to bridge the yawning gulf between the regime and society by developing a 'coalitional method' of rule, by which pliable 'moderate' partners for a controlled social dialogue might be coopted, and responsibility for policy-making thus shared.[16] But this strategy met with continual opposition on the part of the more orthodox hardline element in the political leadership, who, moreover, periodically engaged in provocative incidents (such as the murder of the priest Popieluszko) that undermined whatever shreds of popular credibility Jaruzelski's efforts might have gathered. The hardliners had good reasons to doubt whether such an approach could work – there was, to say the least, something illogical in attempting to develop consultative and participatory methods of rule after having imposed martial law. And, indeed, the new channels for organized participation set up by Jaruzelski remained obstinately lifeless. A decisive factor obstructing change was the mistrust of Jaruzelski shown by the Soviet leadership, especially under Brezhnev and Konstantin Chernenko. The Soviet party leadership provided direct and indirect support and encouragement to the Polish hardline elements. On the other hand, Jaruzelski's persistence on this increasingly futile political course could be explained by the countervailing pressures exerted by Western creditors, who were insisting on some evidence of progress towards political stabilization. Thus the proposed Second Stage of economic reform was put to a freely conducted popular referendum in November 1987 in an attempt to win a kind of democratic authority for, in particular, drastic price increases. But the electorate rejected the proposal, and Jaruzelski was left flailing hopelessly in a web of intractable, mutually irreconcilable, international and domestic pressures.

The Kadar regime in Hungary, to which the Polish reformers had looked for inspiration as a model of political integration through economic reform, was in fact also coming adrift at this time under the impact of economic failure. The pivot of the regime had been Janos Kadar's personal role as a 'centrist' mediator between, on the one hand, the more conservative ideologues and bureaucratic lobbies, and, on the other, the technocratic and reformist economic experts. Kadar himself was not politically inflexible, and recognized the need for change. Up to the

1980s, conflict had thus been contained within the power structure, and many independent-minded intellectuals had been fairly successfully incorporated onto official committees as 'licensed critics' of government policy proposals. Whereas Polish politics was characterized by an unbridgeable gulf between regime and society, since 1956 the Kadar regime had had some success in building bridges with society. But this changed once it was recognized that the leadership had overridden the advice of the economic experts in the 1970s and had taken a fundamentally mistaken path which had led to economic crisis in the 1980s. As a result, the credibility of the whole political structure – the 'Kadar compromise' – and of Kadar personally as leader were called into question. The limits to Kadar's flexibility and understanding of what effective reform required became increasingly obvious. When reformist economists began to advocate a 'reform of the reform' in the early 1980s, Kadar lashed out against them.[17] In so doing, he placed himself firmly on the conservative wing of the party, thus forfeiting the authority and the popular respect he had won in the course of the earlier phase of reform in the 1960s and early 1970s. He also alienated the economic experts, who, particularly after the HSWP Congress in 1985, increasingly defected to the extra-party opposition and, through the medium of *samizdat*, began circulating materials that were highly critical of current economic policy.

At the same time, Kadar's advanced age brought the question of the party leadership onto the agenda: the Kadar era had reached its 'biological limits', as Karoly Grosz, a leading contender in the succession struggle, put it. Kadar began to display the typical characteristics of an authoritarian leader, refusing to retire gracefully. Instead he adopted a tactic of dealing with potential challengers by shifting them to posts away from the centre of power in the party, but this began to backfire on him. For example, in 1987, Karoly Grosz was moved from the powerful position of Budapest Party Secretary to the unrewarding post of Prime Minister. Instead of languishing in the mire of the crisis-ridden economy, Grosz activated the dormant potential of the Prime Minister's office as a vantage point from which to appeal outside the party for new sources of social support, and thus to build the power-base from which to launch a credible challenge to Kadar. Grosz engaged in dialogue with hitherto excluded expert and technocratic groups, and drew up a promising programme for attacking the economic problems. When he presented this programme to parliament in September 1987, his crisp and decisive style made a favourable impression both at home and abroad, contrasting starkly with Kadar, who increasingly appeared tired, ageing and confused.[18] At the same time, the leading figure on the reformist wing of the party, Imre Pozsgay, who had been removed from the government by Kadar in 1982 and put in charge of the Patriotic People's Front (an official, non-party and hitherto toothless body charged with organizing elections and parliamentary activity and staging broad-based social consultations), was using this position to stimulate further public debate on the state of the nation. Increasingly, the party itself appeared to have run out of energy and ideas, no longer a 'vanguard' but the main block on change. The impression of institutional inertia overtaking the party was further confirmed once Grosz achieved his ambition and succeeded Kadar as HSWP General Secretary: he quickly reverted to the authoritarian style for which he had been known when he was the Budapest Party Secretary, and attempted to block further development of the reform debate in an effort to consolidate his power against the growing number of Pozsgay's supporters within the party.

In both Poland and Hungary, the division and drift at the top of the communist party was accompanied by a more far-reaching and irreversible process of decay in the party's 'leading role' in society. The beginnings of the rot can be traced back to the 1970s, when cadre-recruitment policy had downplayed ideological considerations in order to attract a younger generation of well-trained technocrats:

> To most of them the party career was like a job for which they
> expected to be properly rewarded. Accordingly, the ideology of the
> party became a kind of window-dressing ... As a result, the party
> came closer to resembling society, but at the same time one of its
> integrating forces was weakened: the sense of a common political
> mission.[19]

In Hungary in the 1970s, the 'sense of common political mission' had been very much bound up with economic reform. Many able and independent-minded people had been induced to join the party and pursue 'establishment' career paths by the not unreasonable calculation that the cause of reform could be effectively promoted only from within the apparatus.[20] These people were disappointed and felt unacceptably compromised both politically and morally by the failure of the reform, and in the 1980s they provided a substantial constituency in favour of radical change within the party itself. By the mid-1980s, many of them had come to share the conviction that the party's monopoly of power was neither workable nor desirable. They were thus receptive to the idea of a new 'social contract' put forward by the dissident intellectual group Democratic Opposition in June 1987,[21] and were deeply impressed by the proposals for political reform put forward in 1987 in a controversial document entitled *Change and Reform*, written by a group of leading economists.[22]

In order to achieve a decisive break with the past, the party reformists were prepared to extend and thus radicalize the reassessment of the Kadar era beyond the narrowly defined economic field, right back to the roots of HSWP rule in the suppression of the 1956 revolution. This pressure was behind the establishment at the end of 1988 of a historical commission charged with reviewing the entire period of 40 years of communist rule. This concluded that the events of 1956 had not constituted a 'counter-revolution', which was the official description enforced by the Kadar regime that justified the use of force to restore order. Instead it had been a genuine 'popular uprising'. This redefinition undermined the Kadar regime's self-justification as defender of the people's interests. When the HSWP Central Committee itself accepted this finding in February 1989, it signalled not only the final defeat of the conservative-Kadarist faction in the leadership, but also the abandonment of the party's claim of a right to its monopoly of power. The same plenum approved the transition to a multi-party system, opening the way for negotiations with the opposition movements that had sprung up.

In Gierek's Poland, the new brand of apolitical *apparatchiks* was blamed for the loss of party discipline and the spread of corruption in the 1970s; under Jaruzelski, purges were carried out under the pretext of reasserting discipline and central control over cadres, but these also weeded out most of the genuine party reformists who had compromised themselves politically in 1980–81. As a result, the party as an institution proved to be of little use to Jaruzelski in his later attempts to bridge the gulf between regime and society. Under martial law, the party was thrust to one side, or at least found itself sharing power with the military and security apparatus; but when martial law was lifted, it remained irretrievably compromised in the eyes of the Polish people by association with the suppression of Solidarity, and it failed ever to regain its 'leading role'. Membership fell from just over 3m at the end of 1980 to 2m in 1985. Recruitment remained a constant problem, and the share of workers and young people declined dramatically.[23] It was not just moral repugnance that steered potential recruits away from the party; the more immediate incentives to party membership had greatly diminished, since the party was no longer the key channel for access to power, promotion or material reward. Jaruzelski's 'coalitional' strategy sought to revive or bring into being a wide variety of institutions: PRON (the 'Patriotic Front for National Rebirth'), the other political parties, the official trade unions, enterprise self-management. 'At the local level, the party organization was only one among several groups, and was generally not the most active or influential.'[24] At the central level, Jaruzelski preferred to give high visibility to the Sejm (parliament), and set up his own Social Consultative Council as an adjunct to the Council of State.[25]

In both countries, the *nomenklatura* system of party control over society through control over appointments and promotions to all key positions thus underwent a process of dilution and erosion, thereby undermining the central element of the power structure – party control over the economy. The introduction of enterprise self-management weakened the direct control of the party apparatus over the recruitment and promotion of managerial personnel: although the party clearly continued to promote its favoured candidates, it could no longer guarantee their election by the enterprise council, and thus enterprise managers became less directly dependent on the local party apparatus. Moreover, to the extent that economic reforms were introduced, incomes began to depend more on economic performance and less on political connections, centralized redistribution of resources, subsidies, tax concessions and so on. Moreover, as production in the state sector stagnated, the generation of resources for redistribution not only shrank, but new resources increasingly eluded direct party control: the small but dynamic private sector, new cooperative enterprises, foreign-owned firms and joint ventures were the major sources of what growth took place in the economy.[26] Demands for the formal abandonment of the *nomenklatura* system were made increasingly openly in the late 1980s. Its impending demise was signalled in Poland in June 1988, when the PUWP Central Committee approved proposals for a radical restriction of its extent,[27] and in Hungary in early 1989, when the new Prime Minister, Miklos Nemeth, presented to the parliament a new government team that had not received the prior approval of the HSWP Politburo.[28] The system was formally abandoned in Hungary on 8 May 1989.

The final component of the impasse at which Poland and Hungary had arrived by the late 1980s was stalemate in the strategy of social control. Characteristic of both regimes was the striving to dissimulate their essentially coercive nature by efforts to manufacture social consent by what has been called 'covert legitimation',[29] and 'demobilization'[30] of society, and by controlling opposition not only by outright repression, but also by cooptation or marginalization of its most articulate representatives. The economic crisis and increasing incoherence of the political structure undermined the regimes' ability either to repress or to coopt opposition, but they were successful in preventing the upsurge of mass social unrest. The price of this success, however, was a society that had become intractable and ungovernable. The root of the problem in Poland was, of course, the suppression of Solidarity, which Jaruzelski had been quite unable to replace with PRON, or the official unions, or indeed any other channel of communication. 'This is the secret of the Polish situation,' Adam Michnik commented in 1987. 'For six years Jaruzelski has been paralysed by his insistence that Solidarity does not exist.'[31] Solidarity, however, suffered badly under martial law and afterwards, losing its credibility with the exhausted, sceptical and pessimistic population, while failing to win support from a new angry young generation, for whom Solidarity was seen as 'a symbol of cowardice and conformity'[32] because of its leaders' insistence on legalistic, non-violent methods and their search for a way to engage the regime in dialogue.[33]

In Hungary, the population began to show signs of 'reform fatigue', as described in a proposal for a new 'social contract' produced in June 1987 by the intellectual opposition:

The public at large is showing increasing dissatisfaction, but nothing more. They are not thinking about alternatives; they raise no demands ... There are many obstacles to people starting to make demands. First, pessimism; the feeling that economic decline is unstoppable. Then, the discrediting of reforms; since 1979, everything has been 'reformed' but nothing has changed, except the fall in living standards. And the perception of an immovable power elite: it does not matter what 'we' think, 'they' will do what they like anyway.[34]

Notwithstanding the growth and maturation of organized opposition movements from the mid-1980s onwards, Hungarian society remained largely 'demobilized' and atomized, diverting its frustrated energies to the 'internal emigration' of family life, religion, participation in the 'second economy' or escapism of various sorts, including alcoholism. But these forms of adaptation in turn began to act as a constraint on the regime itself: it was not only unable to generate positive support for any of the projects for reform or renewal; its ability even to maintain the *status quo* was threatened. For example, alcoholism, and exhaustion

15

from 'self-exploitation' by moonlighting in the second economy, were a drain on labour productivity in the state sector. The state of public health deteriorated markedly in the 1980s, and this was widely perceived as a result not just of drastic underfunding of the health service, but also of a deeper socio-psychological malaise closely connected with the economic and political crisis.[35] The second economy certainly filled in gaps where the first economy had manifestly failed, but it was parasitic on it: it relied to a significant extent on pilfering and corruption for its access to supplies, and derived high rental incomes from the endemic 'economy of shortage' with which it coexisted.[36] The two economic sectors were not so much competitive as interdependent, and this created a new set of vested interests against reform. The second society was unable to evolve naturally into a civil society that could challenge the official society of state and party, but rather, the two 'have collapsed into each other and reciprocally obstructed each others' normal functions, leading to a fur-ther worsening of our current crisis.'[37]

The path of resistance to reform in Czechoslovakia

In many respects, the breakdown of communist rule in Czechoslovakia is a more straightforward, if not self-evident, story: this regime centred its strategy for maintaining power not on the risky enterprise of domestic reform but on ensconcing itself firmly under the Soviet wing. The regime built up a formidable coercive apparatus, which was justified according to the tenets of traditional Marxist-Leninist ideology, but was ultimately dependent on Soviet backing. When the Soviet Union itself began to depart from those ideological principles and finally abdicated its role of ultimate guarantor of the political order in Eastern Europe, communist rule in Czechoslovakia simply collapsed.

From a comparative perspective, the more complex question to an-swer about the Czechoslovak regime is not so much why it collapsed, but why it was able to sustain the course of intransigent resistance to reform for so long, in contrast to its neighbours in Poland and Hungary. This divergence of paths in East Central Europe can be traced back to the immediate post-Stalin period. The crises of 1956 were the watershed for communist rule in Hungary and Poland.[38] From this point, the imperative of reform impressed itself sufficiently deeply on the respective com-munist parties as to ensure its central position on their political agendas thereafter, albeit with greater consistency for the more thoroughly shocked HSWP than for the more deeply divided PUWP.

16

Czechoslovakia in fact had experienced a mass popular revolt in summer 1953 in Pilsen immediately after Stalin's death, but the restoration of order at this time was effected according to the Stalinist principles still dominant in the Soviet Union, rather than the more flexible approach that became possible once Khrushchev had won the dominant position in the Soviet leadership. The impact of the 1953 revolt in Czechoslovakia was to strengthen the faction of neo-Stalinist authoritarians in the Communist Party (CPCS), whereas in the aftermath of 1956 the influence of such groups inside the PUWP and HSWP was significantly and permanently reduced. In each case, the crises of the 1950s were, in their different ways, a major formative experience of the generation that was still in power in the 1980s, and so they continue to be relevant for understanding the motives and perceptions of political leaders right up to the 1980s.

From the 1950s onwards, groups inclined towards reform, when they emerged within the CPCS, were always embattled and on the defensive. Over time, hardline opposition to reform was further strengthened by experience and by observation of the crisis-ridden progress of reform both at home and elsewhere in the bloc. Thus reforms came to be seen not as a response to crisis, but as its cause. The experience of 1968 was the ultimate confirmation of this for the hardliners of the CPCS; shortly after the Warsaw Pact invasion of the country, a new leadership emerged, dominated by traditional hardliners who were committed to the reaffirmation of neo-Stalinist ideological principles that ruled out even modest experiments with reform. The more pragmatic individuals who survived in the leadership were kept permanently on the defensive.

In 1969 and 1970, there was some evidence that at least part of the new party leadership, including the new party leader, Gustav Husak himself, had expected to be able to follow a 'Kadarist' course, maintaining in public a commitment to continuing the economic reform, albeit one 'cleared of revisionist deposits'.[39] An important conference of economic specialists as late as April 1971 heard the CPCS Central Committee Secretary, M. Hruskovic, reaffirm that outright rejection of economic reform 'would be equal to a step backward in the political, as well as theoretical sense, and would hurt the interests and needs of the Party and the economy'.[40] But economic reform in the wake of the massive application of political coercion was no more possible in Czechoslovakia in the 1970s than it was to prove in Poland in the 1980s. In contrast to Poland, however, both external and internal political conditions favoured the consolidation of neo-Stalinism in Czechoslovakia, with the launching in 1971–2 of a comprehensive purge of reformists from the party. The Soviet leadership had insisted on such a purge, but the energy and ruthlessness with which it was carried out was mainly the contribution of that sizeable cohort of convinced neo-Stalinists, not only in the leadership but throughout the apparatus of the CPCS, which had been shaken but not dislodged in the nine short months of reformist rule. The party purges resulted in a further accentuation of the weight of hardliners by comprehensively eliminating the reform communist faction.[41]

The process of economic recentralization was initially justified not on ideological grounds at all, but as an *ad hoc* emergency response to the profound economic disequilibrium that had been allowed to develop unchecked in the political uncertainty and turmoil of 1968–9; but the momentum of economic recentralization built up as the political purges cut a swathe through the most competent, qualified and reform-minded managerial cadres.[42] Centralization became necessary to ensure the continued operation of the economy under the new, less experienced and less competent, political appointees who replaced them. Finally, in 1972, the word 'reform' itself was officially outlawed from the public vocabulary when the Academy of Sciences issued a comprehensive ideological repudiation of reform economics.[43] Thereafter, even the most modest proposals for 'improvement' of the economic system were open to the charge of fomenting 'creeping counter-revolution', which was held to be even more insidious than the 'open' variant exhibited in 1956 in that it protested loyalty to socialism and pretended only to wish to make it work better.[44] The ghost of 1968 was thus to remain an immovable block on reform in Czechoslovakia, just as the ghost of Solidarity haunted Jaruzelski.

The result of this was to impose drastic constraints on the remaining pragmatic technocrats in the leadership, who were well aware from the start of the likely economic costs of the reform reversal. The leading representative of this tendency was Prime Minister Lubomir Strougal, who attempted to shift Czechoslovakia onto a less inflexible course in the late 1970s. His modest 'set of measures' ventured only to 'improve' the planning system,[45] but the ever-vigilant ideologists, led by Vasil Bil'ak, quickly dispatched this project to oblivion in the early 1980s, when the Polish crisis was used to justify a renewed burst of ideological retrenchment. In 1987, Strougal tried to take advantage of Gorbachev's increasingly explicit reformist example, and once again, but more boldly, advocated economic reform along with a plea for a more conciliatory political approach;[46] but, in the meantime, the CPCS leadership geared itself up for quite a different battle. Husak retired as CPCS First Secretary, but his successor, Milos Jakes, was, if anything, even more inextricably linked to the past two decades of 'normalization': it was he who had conducted the party purges of the early 1970s. It was only a matter of time, therefore, before Strougal was removed from office, as finally occurred in September 1988.

Resistance to reform was thus the pivotal principle of the Czechoslovak regime after 1968; the ability to sustain this course was a product of determined and consistent following-through of the logic of this stance in the organization of power. The extraordinary durability and immobility of the CPCS leadership contrast markedly with the zigzag course and drift in Hungary, and even more so with the recurrent crises and instability of the PUWP. The CPCS had the advantage of clear and uncompromisingly consistent ideological principles, upheld by a disciplined *nomenklatura* and by an extensive internal security system, whose efficiency no doubt owed much to a rather long tradition of bureaucratic administration, predating communist rule.[47] Loyalty to the leadership in the Czechoslovak apparat was guaranteed by the political purges themselves, to which a substantial proportion owed their careers. The introduction of reform for these people meant not merely the likelihood of losing a comfortable, well-rewarded position, but also the psychologically and morally distressing possibility that the former occupants of those positions would reappear in person, demanding their jobs back, and even some retribution for twenty wasted years.

In the economic field, a centralized, closed economy proved to have certain advantages in political terms, which were of course the paramount consideration. In comparison with the reformist regimes, no greater success was achieved in respect of long-term growth rates, efficiency or technological dynamism,[48] but this fact could be concealed by manipulating the statistics and avoiding the prying eyes of Western creditors and of the International Monetary Fund (IMF), to which Poland and Hungary acceded in the early 1980s. What was more significant was that this course avoided the loss of control over basic macroeconomic proportions, and the exposure to the fluctuations and shocks transmitted from the world economy, to which the reformist regimes were patently vulnerable. Czechoslovakia was more restrained in its borrowing in the 1970s than most of its neighbours, and was – in the short term – successful in imposing a centralized adjustment policy in the early 1980s. But it accumulated instead an internal indebtedness, effectively borrowing against its own future by neglecting infrastructural and environmental

19

investment.[49] This did not appear as a problem that the regime had to confront, because information on these issues could be closely controlled by the rigorous censorship, and public discussion stifled in the general atmosphere of political intimidation.

However, centralization had the advantage of putting at the disposal of the regime the vast bulk of economic resources that could be redistributed according to political criteria: to guarantee full employment, to subsidize prices, to satisfy populist concepts of social justice in income distribution, and to sustain the welfare state. Personal consumption and the provision of social welfare may have stagnated throughout the 1980s, but at least the regime could – and did – point to the unhappy lot of the workers in Poland, Hungary, and, of course, Thatcherite Britain to head off criticism of their own record. Those for whom the proper standard of comparison was Western Europe avoided expressing their doubts in public. The regime supplemented outright coercion with the same tactics of 'demobilization' of the population as employed by the Hungarian and Polish regimes, with similarly devastating results on social morale;[50] but because they were not dependent, as was the case in the latter regimes, on a more active role for society in the realization of their politico-economic strategies, they were less affected by the negative consequences.

In short, this was a regime that was virtually immune to the emergence of reformism from within: it had settled into a pattern of 'self-stabilizing oligarchy'.[51] Generational change in the leadership, which was looming on the horizon in the 1980s, was not used as an opportunity for a change of course, and, anyway, the leading representatives of the rising generation in the CPCS, such as Miroslav Stepan, seemed at best to be cynical opportunists with no personal integrity, and at worst callous petty dictators quite prepared to use whatever force would be required to sustain this unsustainable *status quo*. It was in fact Stepan who, as the prime mover of the brutal police repression of Prague students on 17 November 1989, finally was responsible for setting off the process that ended in the collapse of the whole regime.

Serious internal problems generating the possibility of future crises could readily be identified, but it was clear that change in Czechoslovakia would only come with an unprecedented challenge from outside – i.e. from the Soviet Union, which had been responsible for the installation of the regime. Mass revolt was likely to occur only if the people could shake off their apathy and fatalistic submissiveness: they had to believe that change was possible, that the Soviet Union really had withdrawn its ultimate backing from the regime that it had imposed by force twenty years before. This began to occur in 1987, when Czechs and Slovaks read with astonishment the full translation of Gorbachev's speech to the CPSU Central Committee in January, and heard him in Prague in April on the theme of 'our common European home'. Translated into Czech, the vocabulary of *perestroika* echoed uncannily, but unmistakeably, the language of the Prague Spring. This generated hope for change, and encouraged bolder displays of resistance to the Husak regime: for example, in public demonstrations during 1988 – a year packed with highly charged anniversaries – and in January 1989, in which a few thousands participated; or in petitions for human rights and, in particular, religious freedom, which gathered hundreds of thousands of signatures. But uncertainty about how far Gorbachev would allow developments in Eastern Europe to go persisted until 1989. It was not until the demise of the communist regimes of Poland and Hungary had become quite clearly irreversible, without provoking Soviet intervention, that the people of Czechoslovakia felt able to move.

2

THE END OF COMMUNIST RULE

Gorbachev and the limits to change in Eastern Europe

By the mid-1980s, it was already clear that a major upheaval was likely in one or more East European countries as a result of the endemic problems of economic performance and political legitimacy, which had also been at the root of previous traumatic crises of Hungary in 1956, of Czechoslovakia in 1968, and of Poland in 1970, 1976 and 1980–81. It was clear also that no enduring solution of these problems would be possible without a significant relaxation of the political limits imposed by the Soviet Union on change in Eastern Europe. From Stalin through to Chernenko, Soviet leaders had regarded the East European countries practically as provinces of the Soviet Union. As Brezhnev is reported to have explained to the Czechoslovak comrades at the height of the 1968 crisis: 'Your country lies on territory where the Soviet soldier trod in the Second World War. We bought that territory at the cost of enormous sacrifices, and we shall never leave it. The borders of that area are our borders as well.'[1]

Although, after Stalin's death, the Soviet leaders recognized the need for the East European communist parties to take into account 'specific national conditions', nevertheless they expected the East Europeans to fall in line behind their own ideological prescriptions in domestic as well as in foreign policy. They continued to supervise directly the selection of East European party and state leaders, and to insist on close consultation over major policy changes in Eastern Europe. The most explicit codification of the terms of Eastern Europe's 'limited sovereignty' was set out by Brezhnev after the Czechoslovak crisis of 1968, and became known in the West as the 'Brezhnev Doctrine'. This justified military 'assistance' – armed invasion – when the actions of any member of the bloc threatened 'socialism'. The definition of 'socialism' was the prerogative of the Soviet leadership alone, and, until Gorbachev, the terms of the definition left little room for manoeuvre: the preservation of the communist party's monopoly of power and its centralistic internal organization; an economic model based on state ownership of productive assets and the predominance of central planning over market mechanisms; loyalty to the Soviet Union; and dedication to the unity of the socialist bloc.[2]

When and why did Gorbachev decide to jettison the straightjacket in which Eastern Europe had been bound for so long? With hindsight, the 'why' seems easier to answer than the 'when': there is, after all, a compelling logical connection between introducing *perestroika* at home and allowing greater freedom to Eastern Europe. The credibility of Gorbachev's commitment to 'democratization', 'socialist pluralism' and 'new thinking' in foreign policy would be fatally undermined if he continued to deal with Eastern Europe in the same way as his predecessors had done. As Karen Dawisha puts it: 'Gorbachev realized that the Europeanization of the Soviet Union could not proceed without the de-Sovietization of Eastern Europe.'[3] But, until the events of autumn 1989, it was not clear either to Western observers or to the East Europeans themselves that the Brezhnev Doctrine had been abandoned finally and irreversibly. Indeed, for the first two years of Gorbachev's period of office, there was a deafening silence on the subject of Eastern Europe, while thereafter the safest reading of Gorbachev's ambiguous pronouncements seemed to be that the emphasis, but not the substance, of the Brezhnev Doctrine had changed.[4]

With hindsight, we now know that the Brezhnev Doctrine *was* abandoned, and many searching questions have arisen: did we, as outside observers, fail to read the available evidence and to recognize that, in the era of *perestroika*, past Soviet behaviour in the international field was no longer a reliable guide to future behaviour? Or was the cautious approach the only one that could reasonably be defended, given the ambiguity of the evidence?[5] In order to tackle these questions properly, much detailed research needs to be done, since considerable obscurity continues to surround the actual historical events. We need to know at what point the Soviet leadership actually did decide to abandon the Brezhnev Doctrine, and what they expected to happen in Eastern Europe as a result. We also need to address the problem posed by the ambiguity of Gorbachev's public positions: Was this ambiguity a result of incoherence, naiveté and internal contradictions in Gorbachev's thinking on Eastern Europe, or was it a reflection of the strength of the opposition in Moscow and other bloc capitals to the fundamental changes he was advocating? If the former, then outside observers were right to be cautious, given the enormously high potential cost – both for Eastern Europe and the West – of overestimating the limits of Soviet toleration. But, if the latter, then outside observers indeed failed to take into account the relevance for the East European question of the increasing political dominance of radical reformers in the leadership as a whole, and in the foreign policy field in particular, of which there *was* clear evidence from 1987 onwards.[6]

Soviet reformers, including those at the very top who were closely involved in the decision-making, have suggested that the key turning-point in Soviet policy towards Eastern Europe was the CPSU Central Committee plenum of April 1985 – that is, at the point at which Gorbachev took over as party leader.[7] Other authoritative Soviet sources refer to a memorandum confronting directly the question of Soviet-East European relations written by Gorbachev and presented to the CPSU Politburo in late 1986.[8] It is worth quoting at length from Edward Shevardnadze's frank account, presented to the CPSU Central Committee plenum in February 1990:

> ... starting in April 1985, we fundamentally restructured the nature of inter-state ties with them [the East Europeans], abandoned interference in their internal affairs and stopped imposing solutions. But, as our own experience attests, it is easier to change policy than change people. Many leaders in these countries were cut from the same cloth – and it is well known who cut and sewed that cloth. Some of them came to power not without the help of former Soviet leaders, but after April 1985 they could not be removed from power by the current Soviet leadership, since, I repeat, it had forsworn interference in other countries' internal affairs. This was the only correct decision.[9]

The implications of this account are therefore that Gorbachev had already decided to reject the Brezhnev Doctrine when he came to power, and that the ambiguities in his public position in fact reflected both the consistency with which he adhered to the principle of non-interference and the strength of the opposition to change.

This account is largely followed by Karen Dawisha in the second edition of her book *Eastern Europe, Gorbachev and Reform*. Jonathan

Valdez, who has worked closely with Dawisha on this subject,[10] has identified a significant polarization of views within the Soviet ideological and foreign policy establishment dating back to the early 1980s, in the aftermath of the Polish crisis.[11] Open conflict again broke out on the pages of the Soviet specialist press in 1985, shortly after Gorbachev came to power. The public avoidance of the East European question by Soviet leaders for almost two years thereafter is explained by these authors as due, first, to the bitterly controversial nature of the issue, and, second, to the greater priority given at the time to Soviet-US relations as compared with relations with Europe, West or East. However, Dawisha points out that the new defensive orientation of Soviet military strategy and the doctrine of 'reasonable sufficiency' which emerged at the 27th CPSU Congress suggested implicitly that a radical reappraisal of the place of Eastern Europe in Soviet security was likely.

In the course of 1987, the momentum of Gorbachev's domestic reform programme gathered force, and he was subsequently able to bring about substantial changes in both the party leadership and the foreign policy establishment.[12] In foreign policy, the focus of attention began at the same time to shift from the United States to Europe.[13] The culmination of this was the September 1988 Central Committee plenum, which not only saw a decisive defeat for Politburo conservatives, but also brought about a major reorganization of the foreign policy apparatus: the Central Committee Department for Liaison with Communist and Workers Parties in Socialist Countries – the nerve-centre of Soviet control over Eastern Europe – was abolished. East European affairs were transferred to a subsection of the Europe section of the International Department, itself drastically trimmed in size. Now the party's international affairs staff was led by the CC Secretary Alexander Yakovlev, Edward Shevardnadze (the Minister of Foreign Affairs), and others in senior posts who seemed to have thrown overboard almost all the basic premises of traditional Soviet foreign policy. As far as Moscow was concerned, the Brezhnev Doctrine was dead, and it was only a matter of time for the East Europeans to recognize this fact.[14]

Why was it so difficult for Western observers to recognize or to accept the full import of these developments?[15] One major reason may have been the intellectual grip on Western 'Sovietology' of over-deterministic conceptualizations of Soviet politics according to 'models' and 'systems', which engendered resistance to 'paradigm change', very much as identified by Thomas Kuhn in his seminal work on the progress of scientific knowledge.[16] But another reason was Gorbachev's own

unwavering explicit commitment to furthering 'socialism', and his optimistic conviction that this would be the end result of *perestroika*, which
unavoidably generated substantial uncertainty in the minds of outside
observers who took seriously the role of ideology in Soviet politics.
What did he mean by 'socialism'? After all, references to 'socialism'
were also at the heart of the Brezhnev Doctrine. If Gorbachev was mainly
employing references to 'socialism' in a ritualistic way to head off a still
powerful domestic conservative wing, this only served to remind observers of the constraints on Gorbachev, the possibility of his removal,
and the reversibility of the reforms. But if, on the other hand, Gorbachev
really believed that *perestroika* would strengthen 'socialism' in Eastern
Europe, he was plainly naive and ill-informed about the reality in that
region. Radio Free Europe's commentator, Ronald Asmus, put it very
acutely:

> What is increasingly clear ... is that the Gorbachev factor has been
> important in Eastern Europe as a factor in delegitimizing past
> communist rule, but not as a source of intellectual or political
> inspiration. Gorbachev's notion of some form of reform or more
> liberal socialism has evoked little resonance in East European
> societies. Countries such as Hungary and Poland have been practis-
> ing socialist reform and *perestroika* for over twenty years and the
> result has been what one Western observer has termed 'catastroika'.
> Reform socialism, in vogue in the 1950s and 1960s, has long
> become *passé* in much of Eastern Europe as the opposition has
> gone on to develop new theories and strategies for social and
> political renewal along Western lines.[17]

Meanwhile, the impact of Gorbachev's policies was plainly to add to the
likelihood of a major crisis in Eastern Europe, to which he seemed
ill-prepared to respond appropriately on account of his naive optimism.[18]
Whichever way Western observers interpreted Gorbachev on this issue,
a high degree of unpredictability seemed to remain in Soviet policy
towards the mounting crisis in Eastern Europe as late as August 1989:

> As so often in the past, Soviet policy and the precise limits of
> Moscow's tolerance and intolerance are likely to be forged in the
> crucible of a crisis. One of the crucial factors affecting Soviet
> policy calculations may well be what, for lack of a better term,
> could be characterized as the gut instincts of the Soviet political

class ... The degree to which these gut feelings of the Soviet
political class have changed or are in the process of changing is a
question that Soviet commentators themselves find impossible to
answer. It would be premature to assume that the Brezhnev Doctrine is dead once and for all.[19]

The point of presenting the development of Soviet-East European
relations under Gorbachev from these various perspectives has not been
to reach a definitive conclusion, for this would be premature, given the
state of our knowledge of the facts and the need for detailed historical
research. It has rather been to highlight the complexity of the situation.
We know that there was a group of radical reformers in the field of
foreign policy, and we know that they won Gorbachev's support, since
he promoted them. But we know that Gorbachev was never free from the
pressure of intense domestic opposition to *perestroika*, for he spoke more
and more openly about it. Moreover, from late 1988, the process of
Soviet reform 'from above' began to develop a momentum 'from below'
as more radical demands for democracy and for the re-examination of
Soviet history challenged the position of the Communist Party, and as
nationalist movements appeared, which potentially threatened the very
existence of the Soviet state itself. As a result of this, political conflict in
Moscow intensified, perhaps absorbing the Soviet leaders' energies and
diverting their attention from East European developments. Thus they
lost the ability to control the accelerating pace of events in Eastern
Europe, and this would have reinforced the Soviet reformers' case for
deliberately abandoning Eastern Europe altogether.

At any rate, by the summer of 1989, the Soviet limits to change in
Eastern Europe had clearly evolved to the point at which a negotiated
transition to a form of power-sharing between communists and
non-communists had been accepted in principle. It was, as we shall see,
a view shared by the more flexible and pragmatic communist leaders of
Poland and Hungary. It was indeed a massive change from the strait-
jacket of the Brezhnev Doctrine, but it was not to turn out to be an
effective policy in the sense of creating conditions in which reformed
communist parties could retain some influence over the evolution of
events in 1989. The policy disintegrated under the spontaneous pressure
of events in Eastern Europe, as one country after another burst through
the limits of the possible, and communist power disintegrated. Soviet
'policy' now seemed little more than *ad hoc* reaction: no longer defining
the limits, but limiting the damage.

27

Negotiated transition

'The general scenario for negotiating a pact is fairly clear: it is a situation in which conflicting or competing groups are interdependent, in that they can neither do without each other nor unilaterally impose their preferred solution on each other if they are to satisfy their respective divergent interests.'[20] Such was the situation at the end of 1987, when the unavoidable necessity of a new 'social compromise' or 'anti-crisis pact' had become obvious to leading figures in both the regimes and the opposition elites in Poland and Hungary. This involved painful reappraisals of their position by each side, based on the recognition of their weaknesses in the face of revolutionary tensions and the looming prospect of violent social upheaval. The idea of a new compromise divided not only the regimes and their communist parties, but also the opposition in each country.

For the communist party, compromise entailed recognition of the right to exist of groups that had always been perceived as enemies and that they had consistently sought to repress;[21] reluctance to admit the complete failure of their monopolistic rule was compounded by genuine fear of retribution on the part of their aggrieved opponents – the spectre of a 'white terror' was raised by the more resistant factions in the ruling parties. Even those who could claim some credit for advancing the cause of political reconciliation from within the regime were not immune to a sense of guilt for the compromises that they had made with the old regime, and of insecurity as to their future prospects. Taking the initiative in securing a way out of the impasse was thus also in part motivated by the desire to retrieve, as far as possible, their own situation. Two competing concepts of the purposes of negotiation with the opposition were therefore present on the regime side: first, that of *defensive liberalization*, an attempt to control the course and outcome of negotiations in order to ensure the continued dominant position of the communist party, and to 'freeze' the balance of forces in the political *status quo* and block the emergence of further new political organizations; and, second, that of *power-sharing*, based on compromise with the new political movements, which would nevertheless ensure a continued place for the communist party in a coalition in which the opposition would accept joint responsibility with the communist party for managing the economic crisis.[22] It seems likely that most of the leadership of the communist parties in Warsaw, Budapest and Moscow regarded the second concept as the 'worst-case scenario'.

For the opposition (the representatives of the outlawed Solidarity in Poland, and the much more heterogeneous dissident intellectual groups in Hungary), the advocacy of dialogue with the regime involved the abandonment of the high moral ground that had sustained morale during the dismal period of repression and marginalization. It implied abandonment of the strategy of 'new evolutionism' first outlined by Michnik in the late 1970s at the very point at which it seemed to be about to triumph.[23] Michnik's argument had been that there was no point in seeking political change by engaging in dialogue with the communist party or its leadership in the hope of persuading it to reform itself and introduce change from above, since all past experience (in the crises of 1956 and 1968) had demonstrated that such change would at best be shallow and was always reversed over time. Instead, the opposition should attempt to foster change from below, by encouraging and supporting independent social activity and thus the growth of a 'civil society' that would eventually be capable of confronting the regime with an irresistible force.[24] These ideas had decisively influenced the formation of Solidarity in 1980. But now Michnik found himself advocating a return to what looked like the long-discarded so-called 'positivist' strategy of entering into face-to-face interaction with a regime wholly discredited in the eyes of the population, and even forging a 'compromise' with it.[25] As he explained:

Solidarity does not exist just for itself, it exists for Poland. Our union had no right to turn down any chance that presented itself simply in order to keep its hands clean or to please certain radicals … Nobody has a right to turn down a chance because of their grievances, disaffection or prejudice – a chance, of course, born largely thanks to widespread resistance and to widespread support for Solidarity, but also, let's face it, thanks to the very courageous political reorientation of those around General Jaruzelski … That reorientation deserves respect.[26]

Behind this rethinking was the painful recognition by opposition activists of their isolation and of the danger of being rejected by their societies. Underground Solidarity may have continued to enjoy respect, but it was no longer able to rely on a massive response to its calls for election boycotts or token strikes.[27] In Hungary, the 'Democratic Opposition' had always been a small group of intellectuals, regarded as a narrow elite and confined to the capital. Although the influence of their ideas had been gaining ground throughout the 1980s as a result of the quite wide dissemination of *samizdat* literature, they were even less confident than their Polish counterparts of their ability to mobilize mass social support.

Moreover, the idea of a negotiated pact with the regime raised moral questions for would-be democrats: pacts 'move the polity toward democracy by undemocratic means'.[28] What right had a disorganized, marginalized minority of intellectuals to negotiate on behalf of society? The answer they came up with was that it was not a right but a national duty to avert revolution. In Hungary, both the leading HSWP reformists and the opposition activist intellectuals shared a memory of the violence of the 1956 revolution; both sides were impelled to seek dialogue by the fear that, without some kind of pact between the competing political elite groups, another spontaneous, violent social outburst was possible from below, which would once again provoke external intervention to restore order and would ruin the chances of a transition to democracy. A similar concern was evident in Michnik's reasoning at this time:

> The genesis of the totalitarian system is traceable to the use of revolutionary violence ... Whoever uses violence to gain power uses violence to maintain power. Whoever is taught to use violence cannot relinquish it. In our century, the struggle for freedom has been fixated on power, instead of the creation of civil society. It has therefore always ended up in the concentration camp.[29]

The strategy of negotiation and compromise was nevertheless also recognized as being fraught with risk for the opposition: compromise could mean that the old regime would not be fully dislodged from power, and thus that political change might not go far enough to win social support. Then, not only would the basic problem of the government's lack of legitimacy remain, but the opposition itself would be tarnished and further isolated from society. This was the fear expressed by the critics of Michnik and of the strategy of negotiation that appeared in Poland: a new generation of 'angry young men' joined the more long-standing radical opponents of Lech Walesa and his advisors, who had been present in 1980–81 and now reappeared in, for example, the breakaway group 'Fighting Solidarity'.[30] In Hungary, the issue of how far to collaborate with party reformists bitterly divided the Democratic Forum (the self-styled 'centrist' or 'moderate' opposition drawn from the fringes of the establishment) from the other major opposition grouping, the radical-liberal Alliance of Free Democrats, the core of which had been the Democratic Opposition.

Unfinished business – the Polish case

The agreement reached at the Polish Round Table in the spring of 1989 opened a new era with the relegalization of Solidarity. But the agreement rested on a compromise whose assumptions were rapidly undermined by events elsewhere in the region. It is clear with hindsight that the outcome of the negotiations in Hungary in the summer was more satisfactory from the point of view of the transition to democracy. Poland paid the price of being the first: it was not only that the Hungarians were able to benefit by observing the experience of the Poles, but also that the all-important but absent partner in the negotiations, the Soviet leadership, was changing its position in response to the course of events.

At the Polish Round Table, which finally convened in February–March 1989, the two sides, regime and opposition, had shared the basic assumption that the Soviet Union would not permit the PUWP to relinquish ultimate control. The central objective of the opposition negotiating team (led by Lech Walesa and including such well-known figures as Adam Michnik, Tadeusz Mazowiecki and the historian Bronislaw Geremek) was therefore limited to the relegalization of Solidarity as an independent 'social movement' and to securing freedom of the media, thus restoring the *status quo ante* of 1980–81. The Polish regime, on the other hand, sought Solidarity cooperation in elections to produce a more credible Sejm (parliament), and their participation in a new 'coalition' government. But both sides assumed that the PUWP would have to retain ultimate control, at least for the time being, if not permanently.

The compromise agreement signed in April reconciled these competing aims by relegalizing Solidarity in exchange for the opposition's endorsement of elections in which only a proportion of the Sejm seats would be freely contested. The opposition side refused to be inveigled into a predetermined share-out of the 460 Sejm seats between the PUWP and Solidarity, but agreed to an election in which only 35 per cent of seats (161) were fought on the basis of free competition between independent candidates, leaving 60 per cent of seats (276) for the PUWP and its allies, the United Peasant Party (UPP) and the Democratic Party (DP), with the remaining 5 per cent (23) reserved for the officially recognized catholic organizations. But to win any of the seats would require a candidate to win over 50 per cent of the votes cast.

A significant concession by the regime side, facilitating the final agreement, was the establishment of a new upper house, the 100-member Senate, to be elected on the basis of free competition, but enjoying lesser powers than the Sejm. The Sejm and Senate together were to elect by absolute majority the President of the Republic, a very powerful post, according to the provisions of the agreement. The regime side was satisfied with this arrangement because, although the PUWP's dominant position was no longer set in concrete, it calculated that the elections would still produce the basis for sufficient PUWP control, and it was safely to be assumed that Jaruzelski would take the post of President. The opposition assented, *because* the PUWP's dominant position was no longer set in concrete: Walesa saw the agreement as satisfying 'the indispensable minimum for a democratic transformation',[31] and, moreover, the agreement was only to remain valid to 1993. The hope was therefore that new, more satisfactory and democratic, arrangements could be in place for the next elections, due in four years' time. Both sides thus expected a rather extended transition, with room for further negotiation and compromise over the next four years. Both sides were taken aback and unprepared for the results of this deal.

In the first round of the elections on 4 June, Solidarity candidates won by outright majority 160 of the 161 freely contested Sejm seats and 92 of the 100 Senate seats. The PUWP, despite its guaranteed seats, was utterly humiliated: only five of the establishment candidates won outright majorities in their 299 reserved Sejm seats. Worse still, the 'national list' of leading establishment candidates, which the PUWP had put up for 35 of their Sejm seats, was decimated, despite standing unopposed: only two names scraped past the 50 per cent target, and, for the rest, over half the electorate crossed out their names![32]

The PUWP and its allies thus faced a second round of balloting on 18 June in considerable disarray. When the final results were obtained, the Senate was entirely composed of Solidarity candidates with one exception, an independent; in the Sejm, the PUWP had managed to fill its 173 seats (38 per cent), with the UPP filling 76 (17 per cent), the DP 27 (6 per cent) and the Catholic organizations 23 (5 per cent). Solidarity had 161 seats (35 per cent), a minority, but one that enjoyed the distinction of having been won in free competition.[33] The regime thus had secured the largest share of the Sejm seats, but in the process had in fact suffered a terminal moral defeat. Having renounced the right to preserve its position by force, it had failed to replace this by electoral legitimacy.

The astounding and quite unexpected success of Solidarity's candidates immediately called into question the basic assumptions of the Round Table agreement: the formation of a PUWP-dominated government on the basis of these results would be impossible to justify in the eyes of the population. It turned out that the opposition had underestimated its strength, and radical, critical, voices were once again raised, urging the Solidarity leadership to abandon the strategy of gradualism and negotiation in favour of immediate transition to a wholly non-communist government. But, instead, an *ad hoc* renegotiation of the agreement (in close consultation with the Soviet Union) took place around the formation of the new government. Walesa, in an inspired move, persuaded the PUWP's former allies, the UPP and the DP, to switch sides and form a coalition with Solidarity, which then would enjoy a majority of 264 seats in the Sejm. Thus the PUWP's attempt to form a government under General Kiszczak, the former Minister of the Interior, was abandoned, and Solidarity's nominee, Tadeusz Mazowiecki, was asked by Jaruzelski to try to form a government. After protracted negotiations, he put together a government in which the majority of posts (12) would go to Solidarity representatives, while the PUWP and UPP each took four posts, and the DP three posts. In order to satisfy what were then taken to be the minimal demands of the Soviet Union, the PUWP was allocated the key strategic Ministries of Interior and Defence, as well as Foreign Economic Relations, and Transport and Communications.

A final element of the renegotiated deal was the election of General Jaruzelski, by the narrowest of margins, to the Presidency. Again, the motivation of the Solidarity leadership in this matter was to show some deference to Soviet interests in Poland. Inevitably, this renewed the divisions within the Solidarity group of deputies, the vast majority of whom opposed Jaruzelski's candidacy on the wholly understandable grounds that he symbolized in person far too great a degree of continuity with the past; but his election was secured by the abstention or invalid votes of a minority of Solidarity deputies, who were still persuaded by the increasingly controversial arguments for compromise in the interests of stability and of securing what had been achieved. On this basis, a government was formed with sufficient parliamentary backing and popular democratic legitimacy to embark on a drastic economic stabilization programme and to prepare a radical economic reform. But the imperfections inherent in the compromised form of democratic legitimation, and the emergent divisions among Solidarity's deputies in the Citizens' Parliamentary Caucus, gave grounds for doubt about the stability of the political settlement and its capacity to survive the originally envisaged four-year term. The political system itself remained fundamentally in transition.

'Democratic elitism' – the Hungarian case

Negotiations began in Hungary in June 1989, six days after the Polish electoral debacle, and continued in parallel with the negotiations over the formation of the Solidarity government. As the Soviet government's responses to the Polish events revealed the extent to which it was now prepared to let change in Eastern Europe follow its own course, so the possibility of the HSWP pursuing the strategy of contained, 'defensive' liberalization was undermined. It became clear that the best that the HSWP could hope for would be a form of power-sharing with one or more of the opposition proto-parties that had been forming since late 1987. Indeed, by the summer of 1989, it was also becoming clear that the HSWP had shifted its ground: the main division within the party leadership was now between those who expected change to stop at power-sharing, and those who saw the future in terms of open, competitive, multi-party politics, and who accepted the possibility of the HSWP losing power completely. The unique and extraordinary feature of the Hungarian negotiated transition from communist rule was the extent to which the process was promoted and facilitated by the deliberate actions of a faction within the HSWP itself, namely, its radical-reformist wing led by Imre Pozsgay.

On 24 June 1989, when the inevitability of a negotiated 'new social contract' with representatives of the opposition was accepted, the HSWP established a new four-man leadership. The conservative influence of First Secretary Grosz was thus checked by the appointment of Rezso Nyers to the newly created post of Party Chairman, and the inclusion of the reformists Prime Minister Nemeth and Imre Pozsgay, who was to lead the regime's team in the negotiations. The opposition, in turn, organized itself into a 'Round Table' of nine major groups, including the Democratic Forum, the Free Democrats, the new youth movement Fidesz, and representatives of independent trade unions and other newly emerged parties. The official trade unions and social movements demanded a place at the negotiating table too, which thus became a 'triangular', rather than a 'round', table. In contrast to Poland, the Hungarian opposition entered the negotiations with the assumption that wholly free elections were a realizable objective, and this was soon confirmed when the regime's delegation conceded their demand without a fight. Agreement was reached on the new – highly complex – electoral law.[34]

The major point of contention turned out instead to be the proposal for a new, directly elected Presidency. The aim of the proposal, which came from the regime side, was ostensibly to provide a clear focus of legitimate state authority in the transition period, until free parliamentary elections could be held. A freely contested election of the President could be held in late November 1989, and the general parliamentary election would follow in December 1989 or January 1990, allowing time for the parties to organize. But opponents of this proposal saw it as granting too pre-eminent a role to the Presidency in the transition, thus potentially resurrecting the unfortunate pattern of interwar politics in Hungary, when parliament had been passive and manipulated by the dominant personality of the 'Regent', Admiral Horthy.[35]

Moreover, there was a hidden agenda behind this issue, which accounted for the acrimony that it engendered: the obvious candidate for the Presidency was Imre Pozsgay, the party reformer who had built up substantial popular support and had enjoyed high visibility for at least eighteen months during the open power-struggle inside the HSWP. Thus the question of the Presidency became inextricably linked with the role of the HSWP, and of Pozsgay in particular, in the transition and after. This issue divided the opposition between the radicals, such as the Free Democrats and Fidesz, who wanted a decisive break with the past and no concessions that would allow the communists to cling to power, and the moderates, chiefly the Democratic Forum, who were more prepared to cooperate with the HSWP and avoid confrontation. This division was deepened by the knowledge that Pozsgay had in fact been associated with the formation of the Democratic Forum from its beginnings in September 1987; he had personal ties with some of the cultural intelligentsia who had set it up, and he had acted as its protector during the attack by the HSWP leadership in 1987–8.[36] Rumours circulated during the negotiations about a secret deal between the Democratic Forum and the HSWP, whereby the former would be guaranteed the post of Prime Minister in exchange for Pozsgay's accession to the Presidency. The elections might be free, but the HSWP would salvage its position by skilful backstairs manipulations. Relations between the two major opposition groups were soured by these mistrustful suspicions.

The moderate line espoused by the Democratic Forum and the HSWP team prevailed at the negotiations, and the Tripartite Agreement reached in September 1989 included the direct election of the Presidency in advance of parliamentary elections. The radical groupings of the Opposition Round Table did not veto the agreement, but refused to sign it, not only on account of the Presidency, but also because of the failure of the negotiations to cover the questions of the Workers' Guard, the party's private militia, and of HSWP property. The Free Democrats and their radical allies turned instead to mobilize popular support for a referendum on the Presidency, which would allow the people to decide the issue directly. Their success in gathering the required 200,000 signatures on a petition to parliament for a referendum greatly enhanced their public visibility and popularity. When the referendum was held on 26 November 1989 (in place of the planned Presidential election), it resulted in a win – by a very fine margin – for the radicals' position; it also represented a setback not only for the HSWP and Pozsgay personally, but for the Democratic Forum, which had urged the public to boycott the referendum. General elections were thus to be held first, and the constitutional position of the Presidency would be decided by a democratically elected parliament.

Meanwhile, the HSWP's disintegration continued apace as membership began to drift away. A special congress was called for October, with the avowed purpose, promoted by Nyers, of sealing the party's transformation into a modern, West European type of democratic socialist party. But Nyers was also equally anxious to prevent an open split in the party's ranks, and the defection of the more conservative members to form a traditional communist party. Thus the October congress compromised on the redefinition of the identity of the new Hungarian Socialist Party (HSP). This compromise ensured, on the one hand, that large numbers of people, not only in the general public but within the party's own ranks, regarded the change of name as a purely cosmetic operation; on the other hand, Nyers was not able thereby to prevent the defection of the conservatives, who subsequently regrouped under the old name of the HSWP. But the worst mistake of the congress was to dissolve the HSWP altogether and to invite all former members to sign up freely for the new HSP. The leadership seems not to have appreciated the importance of sheer inertia in sustaining the membership numbers of the old party: when given the chance to make a genuinely free choice about whether to join or not, the vast majority of the 720,000 former HSWP members simply left. Only 10,000 answered Nyers' appeal to sign up for the HSP by the end of the month, and it took him much energetic campaigning to bring the membership of the new party up to 50,000 by the end of the year.

The final blow to the HSP came with the October session of the National Assembly, which convened shortly after the party congress to ratify the Tripartite Agreement and to rename the state the Hungarian Republic, excising the word 'socialist' from its title. Now freed from any effective party control, the deputies unprecedentedly took the initiative to further the process of political change by passing legislation outlawing party organizations in workplaces, disbanding the Workers' Guard, and requiring the HSWP/HSP to account for its property.

The date for the general elections was set for the end of March. In the interim, a protracted, and frequently ill-tempered, election campaign was held in free conditions. This period was highly undesirable from an economic point of view, because although the communist government under Miklos Nemeth was still in place, it was nevertheless left dangling without either democratic legitimacy or the possibility of recourse to coercion – and all this in the face of mounting pressures from the IMF to take difficult and highly unpopular economic measures to stave off complete collapse. On the other hand, this protracted period of campaigning had a rather positive effect on political development: the choices facing voters in March were clarified by the pluralization of the political forces. The virtual collapse of the communists as an organized political force afforded the opposition parties the luxury, as it were, of focusing their polemics mainly on each other. Thus the divisions that still remained submerged in Solidarity in Poland were able to come out into the open in the Hungarian context, and as a result the embryo of a pluralistic party-system, already beginning to resemble West European models, was in place by the time of the March 1990 elections. Although a profusion of parties sprang up, there was a 4 per cent hurdle written into the election law, and, even before the elections, two clear alternatives – the Democratic Forum and the Alliance of Free Democrats – had emerged.

The only major problem seemed to be that the election would not produce an overall majority of seats for either of these parties, which would raise difficult questions: Would either party be prepared to invite communist participation in the new government? Or would there be an unstable coalition between the two major parties, whose mutual animosity had intensified in the course of the campaign? These worries were, in the event, put to rest by the results of the two-round election in March-April 1990, which produced a coalition government of the centre-right, comprising the Democratic Forum, which won 165 of the 386 parliamentary seats, the Independent Smallholders' Party with 44 seats, and the Christian Democrats with 21 seats. This government would face an articulate and well-represented opposition from the Free Democrats (with 91 seats) and their close allies, the Young Democrats (with 21 seats). The HSP won 33 seats, but the HSWP was annihilated in the first round, failing to clear the 4 per cent barrier built into the proportional electoral system.[37]

'Velvet revolution' – the Czechoslovak case

In Czechoslovakia, the conditions for a negotiated transfer of power were simply not present in 1989. In fact, for some time, in an unheard-of reversal of roles, leading CPCS ideologists had been issuing warnings to Gorbachev about the dangers of the course he was pursuing, and their unrestrained, open criticism of developments in Poland and Hungary signalled the leadership's determination to continue along the old course. Moreover, no attempts were made to conceal the gearing-up of the domestic apparatus of repression in preparation to support the state in its ever more obvious isolation both from Moscow and from its own, increasingly restive, subjects. Five days of demonstrations in Prague in January 1989 led to the arrest of leading activists of Charter 77, the small, harassed opposition movement, and there followed major political show trials at which they faced charges of 'hooliganism', 'incitement' and obstructing the police. Vaclav Havel received a nine-month sentence. Thus the opposition's appeals for dialogue and negotiation were spurned and indeed looked pathetically misplaced in the face of the regime's intransigence.

But, if at the beginning of the year neither mass revolt nor negotiated reform seemed possible, by the end of the summer developments in neighbouring countries opened the way to radical change in Czechoslovakia. Hungary opened its border to Austria in the spring of 1989, and Austrian TV, which many people in Czechoslovakia are able to receive, showed truly extraordinary pictures of the Iron Curtain of barbed wire being physically dismantled and cheerfully carted away by Hungarian border-guards. Over the summer, large numbers of young East Germans made for Hungary, in order to leave for Austria on route to the Federal Republic of Germany. Until September, the Hungarian government hesitated, abiding by a long-standing commitment to the German Democratic Republic not to permit the exit of GDR citizens from Hungarian territory without an official GDR exit permit. But, by September, the numbers of GDR citizens crowding into temporary refugee camps in Hungary had become a major international preoccupation. Now the Hungarian government, already far advanced in negotiations for the transition to democracy, had no incentive to damage further its domestic popularity by upholding an outdated commitment to the discredited regime of Erich Honecker; on the contrary, it had powerful reasons to court Western, especially West German, approval, in order to secure political and economic support during the coming transition. Thus, on 10 September, the Hungarian government decided to let the East Germans on its territory leave for West Germany, a momentous decision which precipitated the terminal crisis of the Honecker regime. Prague was also affected: the first response of the sclerotic Honecker regime to Hungary's bold move was to ban travel to Hungary, leaving Czechoslovakia as the only country that the hapless East German citizen could visit without elaborate visa negotiations. As a result, large numbers of desperate East Germans now began to pile up outside and in the grounds of the West German embassy in Prague. The citizens of Prague showed open sympathy and voiced encouragement to them. Eventually, the Prague regime, caught awkwardly between the pressures from West and East Germany, had also to concede that there was no alternative to letting the would-be emigrants go. Observing these events, the population of Czechoslovakia began at last to believe that change could really come to their country too.

The opening of the Berlin Wall on 9 November not only spelled the end of the communist regime in the GDR, but also made the survival of the communist regime in Czechoslovakia patently untenable. The paralysis of the CPCS leadership at this point is a truly remarkable testimony to the depth of its political, ideological and psychological immobilism. In fact, there is some evidence that a section of the CPCS apparatus was not impervious to the threat of looming catastrophe for the regime, and sought to engineer a change to avert it. It appears to have been the intention of these *aparatnici* to use an officially permitted student demonstration, which took place on 17 November, as the occasion for an attempted 'palace coup' against the hardline party leadership of Milos Jakes. By instructing the security forces to abstain from immediately arresting leading opposition activists (which had always happened at previous demonstrations), they allowed enough time for an organized opposition leadership to form, with which a renewed party leadership might then conduct controlled negotiations. The CPCS, according to this scenario, would retain the initiative, and the communist regime would be saved by adaptation to the new conditions.[38]

What credibility we should attach to such claims made after the event by now-ousted communist functionaries is yet to be established: the new Czechoslovak Federal Assembly is still investigating the obscure details behind the events of 17 November. But, in any case, the calculations on which such machinations rested betray a complete failure to grasp the basic political fact of the regime's irretrievable weakness, as well as illustrating the characteristic assumption of the *aparatnik* and secret policeman that events could be manipulated and controlled from above. The time had long passed for the application of a strategy of 'defensive liberalization' in Czechoslovakia, as was rapidly exposed in November by the massive, spontaneous force of the popular reaction to the violent police response to the students' peaceful demonstration. Czechs and Slovaks followed the example of their East German neighbours in Leipzig and Berlin, taking to the streets in numbers that were simply beyond the capacity of the coercive apparatus to suppress without calling in the army. And, after November 9, it was clear that the Soviet leadership would not allow the use of the Czechoslovak army for the purpose of internal repression. The CPCS was now undoubtedly on its own.

After a week of mass demonstrations, the CPCS Central Committee met in crisis session, and removed some of the most discredited party leaders from the Presidium (the topmost party body, equivalent to the Soviet Politburo), while retaining the familiar, highly conservative, complexion of the regime. Prime Minister Adamec, who alone among the leadership began to show a readiness to seek dialogue with representatives of the demonstrating population, resigned from the Presidium on 24 November, at the end of this plenum, and thereafter began to act, apparently independently.

Adamec met with the Civic Forum (CF), a spontaneous popular leadership that had sprung up in the course of the demonstrations on the initiative mainly of veteran Charter 77 activists, led by Vaclav Havel, and joined by student activists, as well as representatives of other informal groups and movements that had begun to emerge. Adamec won sufficient confidence from the CF to be entrusted with the formation of a new government, but his proposed new 21-member team, unveiled on 3 December, comprised only five non-communists. This was a grave miscalculation on the part of Adamec, exposing the extent to which even the more flexible personalities in the leadership were captive to the assumption that reformed communist rule was as much as people had the right to expect. After the Polish election debacle and the formation of the Mazowiecki government, following the Hungarian Tripartite Agreement and the opening of the Berlin Wall, the communists in Czechoslovakia simply had no bargaining power at all. Negotiations in these conditions had a rather different role from those in Poland and Hungary: they were entered into in Czechoslovakia at the point at which the two sides were hardly 'interdependent', but instead the opposition, previously small, weak and disorganized, was buttressed by the mass support of the people, whereas the Communist Party had been weakened to the point of dependence on the opposition to avert its complete obliteration and to protect it from uncontrolled acts of retribution by the population.

Adamec was forced to resign under the threat of mass mobilization of the whole society for a general strike. The task of forming a satisfactory interim government was entrusted to Marian Calfa, a CPCS member and little-known legal expert in the outgoing government. His 'Government of National Understanding' was quickly formed and sworn in on 10 December. It comprised a majority of non-communist ministers.[39] Most of the eight communist ministers – including the Prime Minister himself – shortly renounced their party membership.

Thereafter, events in Czechoslovakia were able to unfold freely and with extraordinary speed towards their logical destination. If Poland was paying the price of being first, Czechoslovakia enjoyed the advantage of being last: it achieved more radical change in the personnel of leading political positions than any of its East-Central European neighbours by the end of the year. This was helped along by the behaviour of the CPCS, which, now in retreat, was anxious to salvage some last vestiges of credit by contributing to the orderly and legal transfer of power. It accordingly instructed its deputies in the Federal Assembly to vote for the excision of the clause on the 'leading role of the Communist Party' from the Constitution, and to accept the new Government of National Understanding. A majority of the CPCS deputies were subsequently recalled from the Federal Assembly, and replacements were duly coopted in January 1990 on the basis of *ad hoc* arrangements agreed by the CF and the other parties and movements represented in a Round Table. President Husak himself remained in post only to swear in the new government on 10 December, and he then resigned immediately. Vaclav Havel, the leading figure of the Czechoslovak opposition for nearly two decades and the founder of the CF, was elected by the Federal Assembly as President of the Republic on 29 December 1989.

The new President and government were acutely aware of the dilemma of 'moving the polity towards democracy by undemocratic means', and their first priority was to set the date of free elections, which were to be held on 8 June 1990. The positive legacy of the 'velvet revolution' – the new sense of political efficacy in the population instilled by November's mass participation – came through clearly in the astonishingly high turnout of 96 per cent, recorded in the June elections. These produced a clear majority for the CF and its sister movement in Slovakia, Public Against Violence (PAV), in both houses of the Federal Assembly and in the National Councils of the Czech and Slovak Republics (see Appendix).[40] Marian Calfa, who had by now joined PAV, was confirmed for a second term as Prime Minister, heading a now wholly non-communist government, comprising a coalition of CF/PAV with the Christian Democratic Movement of Slovakia. The new and fully democratic Federal Assembly subsequently re-elected Havel as President on 5 July.

3

THE EMERGENCE OF PLURALIST POLITICS

The ending of the communist parties' power monopoly in East Central Europe opened the way to the free expression of social interests and values that hitherto had been ignored, repressed or forgotten. The challenge for the emergent democratic political order in Poland, Hungary and Czechoslovakia has thus been less one of filling an ideological vacuum in the post-totalitarian society than one of forging a manageable and acceptable pluralistic framework to cope with the surge of fragmented and unstructured interests and values now jostling for a place on the public stage. This framework is necessary in order to mobilize social support for new governments, whose major task is the elaboration and implementation of programmes for the transformation of crisis-ridden, state-socialist economies into effectively functioning market economies. In this chapter, we will approach this complex set of problems by first reviewing the raw material of politics in the three countries: in other words, their political culture.[1] This includes both the available spectrum of values, interests and political ideologies that can be taken up and organized by the emergent new political elites, as well as popular attitudes to participation in politics and more general expectations of the state and government. Then, in the second section, we will review the patterns and problems of party formation in the three countries in order to assess the extent to which the parties currently in existence are likely to prove adequate to the tasks of representing society and of mobilizing support for coherent and workable programmes of action within the framework of democracy.

The raw material of pluralist politics

What are the main sources of political culture? First of all, of course, the shared past historical experience of a society as lived by its members as individuals and groups and transmitted over generations as common memories or ingrained patterns of behaviour. In Eastern Europe, the primary formative experience of the generations now entering active political life was the period of communist rule and its breakdown. During the past four decades, communist regimes made strenuous efforts both to suppress and to reshape the traditional political culture in the interests of maintaining their power. Comprehensive control was imposed over the mass media and education, programmes of ideological indoctrination were introduced, history was rewritten, and creative intellectuals were either suborned in the service of the regime or subjected to intimidation, imprisonment or enforced emigration. These efforts were remarkable both for their intensity and costliness and for their limited effectiveness. The communist regimes in Poland, Hungary and Czechoslovakia never abandoned the family as the primary unit of socialization. Despite the stresses imposed on family life by the very high levels of employment of women outside the home that were required by the ambitious, labour-intensive programmes of industrialization, the family retained its central role in the upbringing of children and thus of transmitting primary values between generations. The family remained an islet of privacy and implicit resistance to the encroachments of the official world of party ideology. Moreover, as communist rule weakened as a result of its manifest failures to deliver its promises of the good life, the dogmatic assertion of official ideology gave way to more pragmatic attempts to draw upon the existing political cultures as a means of stabilizing control by a limited accommodation with genuine social values. Communist rule thus failed to suppress important elements of the political cultures of these societies, but on the other hand it also contributed to preserving or strengthening other elements, such as statism and nationalism, where these could be manipulated in the interests of pacifying society. And furthermore, because communist ideology was associated with national subordination to the Soviet Union and was only ever freely accepted on its own terms by a minority (tiny in Poland and Hungary, larger in Czechoslovakia, but diminishing in strength in all countries as the failure of the system became apparent) it generated among the population a powerful negative reaction, which in turn served to promote aspects of the political culture that had previously been only weakly present.

Popular disbelief in the regime's overt ideological claims was very much deepened by information transmitted by the Western media about life 'over the wall' in Western Europe, from which the regimes proved ever less able to isolate their societies with the onset of detente, increased East-West interaction in the 1970s, and the information revolution in the 1980s. Thus, although active political opposition was, except for brief periods of regime crisis, left to an inevitably small band of exceptionally courageous individuals, a very widespread longing grew up among the people for a 'normal' way of life, understood to be West European-style liberal democratic processes and guarantees of individual freedom – or at least a government that would 'get off people's backs'.

However, communist rule has left an enduring legacy by its rein-forcement of pre-existing traditions, inherited from interwar politics, which will also continue to be an important factor in the development of post-communist politics. Such traditions include technocratic and ra-tionalistic attitudes, which show up in the tendency to search for com-plete, ready recipes and in faith in the application of technical expertise and abstract systemic models; and a corresponding mistrust or lack of appreciation of pragmatism, political compromise and bargaining, all of which are central to 'normal' democratic politics. Communist rule em-bodied an extreme variant of this philosophy of power, but the technocratic-elitist temptation is still implicit in the East European in-telligentsia's sense of its special historic mission to speak for society or to represent its best interests. The demonstrated failure of past piecemeal, *ad hoc* reforms has strengthened the case for the type of all-embracing, systemic solutions on which intellectuals thrive; the current tasks of total transformation and reconstruction of the political and economic systems from scratch, thus provide an extraordinary opportunity for the intelli-gentsia to assume a 'leading role' in politics.

The danger in this is that politics once again comes to be seen as the preserve of experts, which discourages the active participation of the people in policy-making – an involvement that is now essential to legitimating the democratic state and government action. For example, the Polish sociologist Maria Marody has identified the tendency of Poles to see politics as a sphere of activity beyond the reach of ordinary people, involving a 'separate cast of characters' with special qualifications. People see politics as a 'product' not a 'process', as the outcome of decisions made elsewhere and over which the ordinary person neither has nor, it appears, expects to have much control. Marody finds a rather widespread 'sense of helplessness' among the Polish population.[2]

A closely linked legacy is that of paternalism, characteristic to some

45

extent of interwar statist national development programmes, but transformed and deeply entrenched in society by decades of socialist planning and 'welfare-state authoritarianism'.[3] This has fostered a psychology of dependence, summed up by one Hungarian sociologist as an assumption that government is 'for us but without us'.[4] The experience of dictatorial rule has also fostered in the popular mind the habit of dividing rulers from the ruled, into 'them' and 'us', which was natural in the past conditions, but which may not necessarily disappear immediately after the first free elections. People are likely to need time to adjust to the idea that a freely elected government is 'theirs', and that they therefore share some responsibility for its actions. Indeed, people may quickly revert to the pattern of disowning the government when it introduces uncomfortable measures, even if they previously gave it their broad approval at the ballot box. A sense of betrayal of trust may arise, rapidly eroding the legitimacy of the government and of the democratic system itself.

Post-communist societies are all, in varying degrees, risk-averse in both the political and the economic senses. The pattern of 'internal emigration', of escape from politics to the weekend country cottage or to the vodka bottle, could prove quite hard to break, especially in a period of economic dislocation and of gathering pessimism about the prospects of a rapid improvement in conditions of life. To be sure, recent East European history – in particular the Solidarity period of 1980–81 and Czechoslovakia's 'velvet revolution' – demonstrates the heroic capacity of these societies on occasion to throw off the blanket of mass apathy; and, on a more mundane level, the flourishing 'second economy' in Hungary, the private agriculture in Poland, and the black market everywhere, are pockets of determined entrepreneurship and individual initiative whose importance should not be forgotten.

Nevertheless, in the cases of Poland and Hungary in particular, there seems to be a rather low level of general interest in political life, as evidenced by relatively low, and declining, turnouts at elections. In all three countries, the numbers actively involved in day-to-day building of the new parties and movements are still quite limited. Political activism in the West is also, of course, the exception rather than the rule, and we should avoid imposing on Eastern Europe unrealistic standards that are derived from an idealized notion of democratic citizenship which is not evident in practice elsewhere. However, there are specific features of this phenomenon in Eastern Europe: although indifference to political participation through the medium of parties may to some extent reflect a rather general, post-industrial aversion to hierarchical, bureaucratic forms of participation and political self-expression that are found also in Western Europe, in Eastern Europe this is greatly intensified by popular mistrust of the party form *per se*, derived from past experience of 'The Party'. Thus the new parties strive to avoid describing themselves as parties and to structure themselves as far as possible loosely and informally, as we shall see in the following section. Behind this lies a more general mistrust and rejection not just of formal organization but of power itself, reflecting a profound disillusion and scepticism of politics as a morally corrupt, dirty business to be shunned by respectable, decent people. This also affects attitudes to pluralism and opposition. People seem to expect the national unity achieved at the climax of the struggle to end communist rule to continue in post-communist politics, and thus seem neither to understand nor to approve the bi-party or multi-party competition evolving from within the new political leadership. A major task in retrieving the political culture of Eastern Europe is, in the words of Vaclav Havel, the 'rehabilitation of politics' – the development of an appreciation of the constructive potential of institutionalized conflict and competition for power.

A further major factor shaping the values, attitudes and expectations that make up political culture are economic interests and the social structure. The period of communist rule has made a dramatic impact here, sweeping away whole strata of the population in the process of expropriating private property in the means of production. This involved the physical destruction by emigration or proletarianization of the old landowning and 'bourgeois' classes, the transformation of the independent professions into servants of the state, and a great expansion of the class of industrial workers in the process of accelerated large-scale industrialization. But the modernization of the economies and societies of Eastern Europe has been only partial, and, in the more recent period of economic crisis, in some respects has gone into reverse. Agriculture in particular was systematically neglected. The collectivization of agriculture was very limited in Poland, and in the other countries peasants retained private plots, which accounted for a disproportionate share of total food production. The class of small, impoverished peasant farmers thus remains as a potent reservoir of traditionalist attitudes and especially of religious values.

Outside the Czech Lands (the provinces of Bohemia and Moravia), which were industrially the most highly developed part of the Austrian empire, the industrial working class has scarcely had time to develop into that 'hereditary proletariat' in which Marxists placed their hopes for the social support-base of communist ideology. It has retained strong links with the countryside; as a result of such pressures as the failure of housing construction to keep pace with the growth of the new working class in the burgeoning industrial centres, a common pattern has been the combined worker-peasant household, where the husband commutes to the city to work in industry while his wife remains in the village to tend the family's small farm or private plot.

None the less, despite this degree of overlapping industrial and agrarian lifestyles and interests, the deep rift between urban and rural life that was so marked in interwar society and politics remains as one of the most potent divisions in post-communist politics.[5] The communists' ideologically based neglect of agriculture and the marginalization of rural society means that the city is still the main locus of opportunity for self-betterment, offering better facilities for living, acquiring consumer goods and services, education for one's children, an easier, more comfortable existence, and access to political power. Traditional rural resentments and populist mistrust of city life as godless, alien, corrupt, privileged and parasitic on the honest, hard-working countryside, idealized as the embodiment of true national values, have rapidly resurfaced in the context of open, competitive politics.[6] This is evident in Hungary, where the deep ideological fault-line between 'urbanists' and 'populists' that was prevalent in interwar intellectual debates has once again become a major reference point for the new parties. And a similar division is appearing in Poland as the unifying force of Solidarity gives way to the search for channels of expressing the real diversity in society and for sources of social support for the new political forces. In all three countries, moreover, the urban-rural rift is a source of regionalist tensions, and it underlies the national conflict in Czechoslovakia, the Czechs constituting a more highly urbanized, industrial and secular society, whereas Slovakia is markedly more rural, agrarian and traditional, with the Catholic Church exerting a stronger influence.

In the process of articulating this real social division, almost inevitably elements of anti-semitism have re-emerged, since historically in Eastern Europe the vitality of urban economies and culture derived in large part from the contribution of the Jewish minority. This particularly unpleasant throw-back to the political culture of the interwar period presents a major challenge to democratic politicians. Its re-emergence – despite the terrible decimation of the Jewish communities of Eastern Europe in the course of the Second World War and the further losses through emigration during the communist period – is a symptom of the current crisis of modernization that has reappeared, once again facing these societies with a fundamental choice between, on the one hand, an open, tolerant pluralism, which is the necessary condition of change at home and of international reintegration with the West, and, on the other, the cheaper, easier gratifications of a narrow, inward-looking, parochial traditionalism, a pattern familiar from the pre-communist past of the region.

A further important feature of the social structure of Eastern Europe with relevance for its political culture is its current fragmentation and instability. After the social, economic and political dislocation brought about by the initial communist 'revolution from above' in the late 1940s and early 1950s, the societies settled for some decades into a form of state corporatism, structured around the bureaucratic sectoral organization of the industrial sector into large, monopolistic enterprises. The interests of the workers were bound up with their enterprises to a much greater extent than in the West, since access to flats, recreational facilities, social welfare benefits, and even scarce consumer goods was to a great extent conditioned by the resources of the enterprise, which in turn depended on its bargaining power in the centralized allocation of resources according to the political preferences of the regime. The interests of workers as a class were thus cross-cut by their specific interests as employees of more or less highly favoured industrial branches and enterprises. Improving one's material position was most effectively ensured not by participating in collective action in trade unions, which never acted as pressure groups in the Western sense, but individually, either by seeking employment in a more powerful enterprise or by moonlighting on the second economy.[7] Either way, one bettered oneself by one's own efforts.

As the economies slid into decline, state enterprises became ever less able to guarantee the expected wages and benefits, and workers diverted their efforts ever more to secondary earning. In Hungary and Poland, the importance of the second economy in maintaining, or preventing too sharp a decline in, living standards was recognized by the regimes, and, during the 1980s, the sphere of legalized, or tolerated semi-legal 'grey', private economic activity expanded markedly.[8] The result of this was not the formation of a cohesive new class of small entrepreneurs; this was blocked by the continuing insecurity of the private sector. Most people kept their job in the state sector and the secure minimum income that came with it. Corruption of local officials and pilfering of state property to obtain materials, equipment and time, led to a high degree of interdependence with, if not parasitism on, the state sector. The result in terms of the structure of interests was thus to further atomization and disintegration, processes that will, moreover, accelerate in the period of economic transition, in which whole sectors of the state economy will undergo bankruptcy and closure, demonopolization and privatization. In these circumstances, we must expect to see an unprecedented degree of social destructuring, volatility and fluidity, before new, cohesive, broad interest groups re-establish themselves on the basis of the market economy. This will pose exceptional problems from the point of view of mobilizing stable sources of political support for the new parties and governments. It has to be recognized that, in these circumstances, emotional appeals will prove far more effective and meaningful than 'rational', interest-based appeals for party support.

Let us now focus on the ideological spectrum emerging in Eastern Europe. In the aftermath of failed communism, the most potent ideological force to re-emerge is *nationalism.* This is inevitable given the historical importance of the question of national identity in the exceptionally complex, multinational patchwork of the East European region, and the vital role of national pride in stimulating popular resistance to, and finally rejection of, Soviet-imposed communist rule. People are looking back to the precommunist past to rediscover their national identity, to find positive symbols and historical hero-figures as sources of pride and common allegiance, and to retrieve authentic national models for the political institutions that must now be re-created. But nationalism has played an ambiguous, at times disastrous, role in Eastern Europe's political development, appearing as a form of fascism, exhibiting the parochial, intolerant, anti-semitic traditionalism that has yet to be firmly laid to rest in the region.[9]

However, in the current circumstances, not only can nationalism not be simply ignored or suppressed, but its potential positive contribution to the democratic political transformation of Eastern Europe should be recognized. Nationalist politics provides the emotional appeal that can win wide allegiance from a fragmented, atomized society, overcome the deep sense of humiliation inherited from the experience of communist dictatorship, and provide convincing reasons why people should once again be asked to tighten their belts and to display political altruism. The key moment in the establishment of secure foundations for democracy in Eastern Europe will thus be the emergence of new nationalist political leaders who are able to forge from the rather rich mixture of national, Christian, peasantist and traditional values that abound in the region a modern form of Christian Democratic movement which will straddle the urban-rural divide, marginalize anti-semitic and neo-fascist attitudes, moderate the more dogmatic and divisive tendencies of Catholic conservatism, and channel nationalist aspirations in an open-minded, outward-looking direction.

The prospects for this are far from bleak, even though the current period of crisis and transition is raising fears of a repetition of the less happy interwar political patterns. But the international environment – always a crucial determinant of East-Central European politics – is vastly more favourable for democracy today. The democratic development of Western Europe in the postwar period now has an impact on East Central Europe not only as a positive example to be learnt from, but also, more directly, a supportive influence – as West European political parties, particularly the Christian Democrats and Social Democrats, seek out their counterparts in the East in order to encourage them and to exert influence over their evolution.

More important still, some of the intractable problems that were at the root of Eastern Europe's interwar problems have been resolved: above all, state borders are now finally fixed, and the West will resist firmly any attempts to reopen border questions. The 'German question' has been solved in a way that is supportive of stable democracy. The redrawing of Poland's borders after the Second World War gave rise to an ethnically highly homogeneous state, which should have removed the original causes of the deformation of Polish nationalism. In Hungary, nationalism was traditionally strongly irredentist, making vast territorial claims against three of its four neighbours. Although concern for the fate of Hungarian minorities abroad remains a live political issue in Hungary today, irredentism seems to have shrunk to very much a minority preoccupation. This is largely due to the countervailing strength of popular pride in Hungary's 'return to Europe' over the past decade. Communist politicians in the Kadar period came to appreciate the benefits of closer economic integration with the West, and won some popular credibility at home in the midst of economic failure by showing an independence from the Soviet Union in international affairs, culminating in the opening of the borders to allow the free emigration of East German citizens in September 1989, which precipitated the collapse of the GDR and subsequently of Soviet rule in Eastern Europe. The costs of forfeiting this reputation have now to be borne in mind by any would-be irredentist politician in Hungary.

Nationalism in the case of Czechoslovakia presents greater difficulties. The intractable interwar problem of the German minority in the

Czech Lands no longer exists, owing to the expulsion of virtually the entire German population immediately after the end of the war. But Czech-Slovak national tensions have revived with the reappearance of a vigorous Slovak nationalism, which also impinges on Slovak relations with the 600,000-strong Hungarian minority in Slovakia, and thus on relations with the neighbouring Hungarian state.

Slovak nationalism derives in part from understandable frustration at 'Prague centralism' under both the interwar republic and the communist regime, which denied Slovaks the promised degree of self-government. It is also provoked by the patronizing tone in which Czechs tend to address Slovaks as 'younger brothers'. Czechs, for their part, overact all too readily to any manifestation of Slovak assertiveness as potentially 'fascist' and a threat to the integrity of the state – a reflection of their bitter memory of 'betrayal' in the 1938–45 period, when Slovak separatists enlisted Nazi support for the establishment of an independent Slovak Republic. And, it has to be said, the more extreme variants of Slovak nationalism reappearing today do indeed lend themselves to such accusations, being not only openly separatist and deeply conservative, but also marked by xenophobia and intolerance of the rights of minorities, such as Hungarians and gypsies. However, opinion-poll evidence suggests that only 5-10 per cent of Slovaks favour outright independence; the vast majority thus still seem to appreciate the practical disadvantages of separate statehood for such a small nation, while at the same time favouring radical reform of the federation, which is by no means necessarily against the interests of the Czechs themselves or of the development of democracy. The biggest obstacle may therefore turn out to be, not irreconcilable incompatibility of the goals of the two nations, but lack of experience among the respective national leaderships in the political techniques of hard-bargaining and compromise that federal reform will entail.

If the 'democratic revolutions' of 1989 had any ideology, it was that of *liberal democracy*, thus demonstrating the extent to which democratic political culture in East Central Europe developed in reaction against communist rule. But it has to be recognized that the social support-base of liberalism remains weak and ill-defined: given the restricted development of the private sector in the economy, it is dependent on a rather limited segment of the intellectuals and the urban professionals. Although there is widespread popular support for the general values of individual freedom, democracy and the market, the abstract universalism of liberal ideology in its undiluted form may not be enough to satisfy popular needs for a political myth capable of generating a sense of common purpose that will compensate for the stresses of the coming economic transition. The general point is eloquently expressed by Maurice Keens-Soper:

> Democracy in Western Europe turns upon the existence of strongly cohesive collective identities which are centred in nationalism … Liberal democracy has almost everywhere been parasitic on nationalism. Democracy possesses no theory or force of its own capable of either generating or explaining the very ties of attachment upon which its workings in practice depend. Without a 'body' whose politics can be democratically ordered, party-politics contains no substantive coherence or principle of continuity.[10]

The overt 'Western' orientation of proponents of liberalism is both a strength and a weakness: on the one hand, overt commitment to Westernism, or Western models, holds out the attractive promise of achieving the longed-for 'normal' politics of the West, and especially its economic prosperity, as idealized in the minds of East Europeans. On the other hand, the implementation of an undiluted liberal strategy in the economic transition could easily appear as a brutal policy of 'social Darwinism' and the glorification of individual self-interest, undermining deeply held values of community and national identity. Perceived Western indifference to, or lack of support for, the transition could thus generate a popular reaction both against the West and against liberal values in general, comparable with the populist backlash we have seen in some Latin American countries. Liberalism must strengthen itself by tapping into national moods and aspirations, just as nationalism needs an infusion of liberal values if it is to be compatible with the emergent democratic framework.

Socialism as an overt ideology has been profoundly, if not fatally, weakened by association with communist rule and by the failure of the economics of central planning and state ownership. A deep, almost allergic, reaction has developed to the notions not only of 'communism' but more broadly of 'socialism' and the 'left' as utopian, unworkable and inherently opposed to freedom and democracy. At least in the transition period, it is hard to see a major place for socialist parties, given the uncongenial nature of the tasks in the economy of marketization and privatization for socialists. However, the period of communist rule did have an impact on social attitudes in terms of high expectations of

53

welfare provision, protection of the standard of living, and job security that have to reckoned with. To some extent, such expectations have been tempered in Poland and Hungary by popular knowledge and under-standing, accumulated from experience over the past decade, both of the real implications of radical economic reform for the standard of living and job security, and of the inability of these economies to fulfil the promises made by the communist regimes in terms of welfare. In Czechoslovakia, where information about the true state of the economy had not been freely available for decades, 'welfarism', aspirations to a 'Swedish model', and unrealistic optimism about the ease of transition to a market economy are more in evidence, but opinion polls also showed a high degree of willingness to undergo economic retrenchment for a period of one or two years in order to bring about necessary changes. Observation of the traumatic experience of East Germany in the process of economic unification with the Federal Republic has had a sobering impact on expectations. This rather pessimistic popular mood makes it more difficult for the left to mobilize support for a party committed to an alternative economic policy, since most people do not appear to believe that a credible alternative exists. Nevertheless, welfarist demands are likely to resurface through the activity of interest groups. Although at present such demands are unlikely to provide the basis for the revival of socialist parties, none the less periodic *ad hoc* challenges to the new governments can be expected, which could be all the more difficult to deal with on account of their spontaneity and their lack of integration in the party-political spectrum.

Movements and parties

The first point to be made about political parties in post-communist East Central Europe is their sheer numbers – indeed, we could fill the limited space available here simply by listing their names.[11] This profusion is encouraging evidence of political vitality and of the desire to participate in politics, which should be set against the rather pessimistic emphasis of the points presented above. It recalls the interwar period, which was similarly characterized by the presence of an elaborate multiplicity of parties. Indeed, many of the newly emergent parties rest their appeal on claims to historic continuity with parties that existed in the interwar or immediate post-Second World War periods. Nevertheless, the new pro-portional electoral systems of Hungary and Czechoslovakia have built-in minimum-percentage 'hurdles', which have successfully reduced the number of parties represented in the national legislatures (see Appendix). So far, the so-called 'historical' parties have proved markedly less successful in organizing themselves, gathering members and winning votes than either the wholly new movement-parties that dominate the first post-communist assemblies and governments, or even the successors of the communist parties and their allied 'fellow-traveller' parties. The picture remains one of great fluidity, so the purpose of this section is to survey only the major parties that have come into existence in the first eighteen months of the post-communist period.

The most important type is what we shall call here the 'movement-party', a transitional form of political organization that can be expected to undergo substantial evolution towards the more traditional party forms that are found in developed democracies. This term covers the Solidarity Citizens' Committees in Poland, the Civic Forum (CF) in the Czech Republic, and Public Against Violence (PAV) in Slovakia. Although the founders of the Democratic Forum and the Alliance of Free Democrats in Hungary seemed at first to be aiming at creating broad coalitional movements rather than parties, the somewhat extended process of relatively unobstructed political pluralization from late 1987 fostered the development of more differentiated, coherent, party-like identities. Moreover, their creation was largely the product of elite initiatives, rather than the mass pressure that was so important in the original formation of Solidarity, the CF and PAV.

The key characteristics of the movement-party are its broad coalitional form, its vague, non- or anti-ideological and strongly moralistic programme, and the informality of its internal organizational structure. Movement-parties first emerged as the representatives of 'civil society' in mass protest against totalitarian communist rule. The central leadership role was assumed by a core of long-time former 'dissident' activists, who presented themselves at the moment of breakdown of communist rule as negotiating partners with the old regime, and who provided a focus for the mobilization of broad-based, spontaneous popular pressure against communist power. Subsequently, the organizational demands posed by the elections contributed to the first steps in their development as quasi-political parties, but, after the elections, when confronted with the new task of exercising power, internal strains have appeared both within the leaderships and among leaders in government, parliamentary deputies and grass-roots activists. The unmanageable variety of ideologies, interests, personalities and general political objectives that they embrace lies at the root of the instability of the movement-parties, and both external observers and the participants themselves accept the inevitability of reorganization and realignments in future.

The archetypal movement-party is Solidarity in Poland, which was first established in the crisis of 1980–81 as an unprecedented challenge to communist rule, gathering an estimated 10m members.[12] From its origins, Solidarity studiously resisted identification as a political party: it was an 'independent trade union', disavowing any interest in taking power in the state. The question of collaboration with the communist authorities in drawing up a programme for 'national renewal' and economic reform was highly contentious within the movement. The obvious reason for refusing to accept the designation 'party' was that this would have challenged the communist party, inviting immediate repression. Resistance to power-sharing was also based on a well-justified scepticism about the motives of the communist authorities: Solidarity recognized the dangers of being emasculated, as the workers' councils had been after 1956, and of losing popular credibility by association with a painful programme of economic recovery. Participating in government would have led to confusion and strain in a movement whose avowed role as a trade union relied primarily on the support of workers in the shipyards and large enterprises in traditional industrial sectors, who would be the first to suffer from any conceivable economic reform.

But there were also deeper, more emotional, factors at work alongside these pragmatic considerations: for a large section of the members, traditional political objectives were in fact less significant than the unique opportunity for personal and national self-expression that Solidarity provided. As many observers have noted, Solidarity was 'a conviction and a state of mind rather than an instrument of collective action'.[13] It represented general national and religious values, rather than specific, partial interests: while it was fired by the democratic ideals, it was a *pre-pluralistic* movement, based on an assumption of social unity and harmony. 'It had also the aspect of a moral crusade. Its members and leaders sometimes thought primarily in moral or religious categories of the struggle of good against evil.'[14] To this extent, it bore a stronger resemblance to the 'new social movements' appearing at the same time in Western Europe than to a trade-union movement in the sense understood in the West.[15] Its internal organization was 'horizontal' rather than hierarchical; questions of internal discipline and leadership accountability were contentious and remained unresolved: it was 'an incoherent mass movement, a kind of social avalanche or political landslide which could not be meaningfully controlled and guided'.[16]

The legacy of this formative period is evident today – although in very changed circumstances – which accounts in part for the emerging strains within the movement. On the one hand, the new demands on Solidarity made by participation in elections and government have brought out latent conflicts in the leadership over strategy and policy. On the other hand, the core of the leadership and Solidarity activists, shaped by the experience of 1980–81 and the long years underground, now confront a different society, more sceptical and pessimistic about the way out of the crisis. Polish people are less amenable to the unifying force of general moralistic appeals, and more fragmented into a plethora of confused and sharply conflicting interests; but they seem not yet to be ready to accept either the necessity or the desirability of political pluralization.

Solidarity has revived as a trade-union movement, with 2-3m members. A separate set of 'Citizens' Committees' was formed hastily to cope with the task of organizing political activity at all levels. At the centre, around the personality of Walesa, is the Citizens' Committee, first formed in December 1988 as an advisory group of about 130 key intellectuals and underground activists, who were coopted to support Walesa's team in the 1989 Round Table negotiations. It then drew up an election platform for the June 1989 election and approved lists of parliamentary candidates. These were nominated by local Citizens' Committees that sprang spontaneously into existence, comprising both former oppositional activists and new, previously inactive, individuals. After the election, Solidarity's deputies formed a 'Citizens' Parliamentary Caucus' to coordinate parliamentary support for the Mazowiecki government. Relations between these various parts of the movement were only loosely defined, and conflicts rapidly emerged both among and within them.

First of all, because the election was basically a plebiscite against communist power, Solidarity's programme was extremely general, designed 'as much to convince the public to take part in the elections as to persuade them to vote specifically for Solidarity's candidates'.[17] Candidates stood as 'individual citizens' rather than as representatives of particular interests or programmes. As a result, Solidarity's parliamentary deputies span a spectrum of 'social democrats, worker self-management activists, liberal adherents of the free market, agrarians, centrist unionists, Christian democrats and right-wing conservatives'.[18] Internal conflicts were inevitable once the Mazowiecki government's economic programme began to be implemented; but an underlying factor accelerating the process of coalescence of factions from mid-1990 was the problem of Walesa's role. Walesa had chosen not to take a formal state or government post. He expected instead to rely on his personal charismatic authority both to secure a decisive influence over the Mazowiecki government and to enable him to act independently of it, as a supra-political representative of society as a whole, or even against it when, as occurred in the summer of 1990, the economic stabilization programme produced signs of a popular backlash. Dissatisfied with the limited effectiveness of his informal influence, Walesa decided to stand for the Presidency, fracturing the Round Table agreement of 1989, which had left Jaruzelski in this post. This challenge deeply divided the movement. Walesa exerted pressure on the Mazowiecki government to accelerate political reform, and openly criticized its alleged elitism, lack of contact with society and excessive willingness to compromise with the remnants of the communist authorities. Walesa's actions generated conflicts within the parliamentary caucus between his supporters and those of the government. The central Citizens' Committee became increasingly a personal power-base for Walesa as he summarily dismissed prominent government supporters from key posts in it. The division at the top was not only a matter of personalities; it reflected as well two competing concepts of the role of Solidarity in the transition period. Walesa drew support from deputies and political activists associated with more strongly nationalist and Christian groupings and proto-parties, who felt that they had been passed over or excluded by the Mazowiecki team, and who therefore supported further pluralization as a means of obtaining greater influence and visibility; the supporters of the government saw Solidarity's role as a unifying force behind the government as it introduced extremely radical economic measures.

Meanwhile, the local Citizens' Committees were drawn into the political struggles at the centre. Walesa's supporters urged the committees to resist attempts by Mazowiecki's allies to draw them into a federal structure, which would facilitate more institutionalized coordination of the movement behind the government. This was attacked as a dangerous attempt to hijack the movement, creating a new 'monoparty', dominated by the government's supporters, which would stifle pluralism and the newly emerging political parties. The function of the Citizens' Committees, Walesa insisted, was to be 'schools of democracy' and 'incubators' of new parties, rather than themselves to develop into a party.[19] Considerable differences emerged on these points among the local Citizens' Committees, and, at a crucial national conference of their representatives at the end of June 1990, a series of rather contradictory resolutions were adopted: they agreed to hold periodic consultative conferences, but these were to have no executive authority over local committees and would not constitute a national representative body; they also voted in favour of developing federal structures within the Citizens' Committee movement, and resisted Walesa's proposal to open their doors to collaboration with other new parties.[20] The local committees thus demonstrated their independence from both of the major leadership factions, and they remained only informally linked to the parliamentary caucus and the central Citizens' Committee.

Walesa's campaign for the Presidency propelled the leadership factions towards greater organization of their respective supporters, splitting the movement into what appear to be two embryonic alternative parties, although, characteristically, neither describes itself as a party: the Centre Alliance was formed on 12 May, organized primarily around Walesa himself (but not in fact led by him); and the Citizens' Movement-Democratic Action (ROAD in its Polish acronym) was set up in response on 16 July, grouping many of the supporters of the Mazowiecki government.[21] Both are still coalitions, but with increasingly distinctive identities. The Centre Alliance is essentially Walesa's personal following. But it also identifies itself as 'right' or 'right of centre', appealing to a range of populist, traditionalist, nationalist and Christian-Democratic tendencies. It has found clear allies in small proto-parties called the Christian-National Union and the Liberal-Democratic Congress. Walesa insists on labelling (or rather, in the Polish context, stigmatizing) his opponents in ROAD as 'left'. ROAD's leaders, however, reject the relevance of the left-right division as an artificial imposition of prewar categories onto a totally different situation. Zbigniew Bujak, a leading figure in ROAD, prefers to describe ROAD's orientation as 'West of centre', projecting a liberal, progressive, secular and 'Westernizing' self-image, which is contrasted unfavourably with the Centre Alliance's alleged primitive, inward-looking, traditionalist nationalism and anti-semitic tendencies.[22] ROAD supporters and sympathizers among the parliamentary deputies have left the Citizens' Parliamentary Caucus and have formed their own caucus under the title 'Democratic Union'. The task of converting these broad intellectual-cultural currents and personal animosities within the new political elites into the bases of organized parties with mass electoral appeal lies ahead.

The CF in the Czech Republic and PAV in Slovakia exhibit many similar features to the Solidarity Citizens' Committee movement, although of course they have a much shorter history, dating, strictly speaking, from the events of November 1989. But their spiritual roots can be traced back to the formation of Charter 77 and to more recent oppositionist activities, and the philosophy of Vaclav Havel has had a formative influence on them. Strong personal and intellectual links existed between the opposition activists of Poland and Czechoslovakia in the 1980s, leading to a cross-fertilization of ideas, which helps account for some of the similar features in the respective movement-parties. For a large proportion of the activists in Czechoslovakia, an emphasis on morals, individualism and spontaneity and a suspicion of power, hierarchy and formal organization are central values and attitudes with much more salience than the various explicitly political ideologies that coexist within the movements. Like Solidarity in its early days, they often adopt the tone of 'moral crusaders'. But rapid internal changes have been under way since the June 1990 election: differentiation of factions has begun inside the CF, whereas PAV has developed a more coordinated internal structure.

The two movements sprang up simultaneously in November 1989 quite independently and at first in mutual ignorance. Although once they had made contact the extent of common ground made close cooperation obvious, the very different environments of the Czech and Slovak Republics have led to diverging emphases and to not a little strain in their mutual relationship. PAV almost from the first faced potent rivals in the Slovak Christian Democratic Movement and, later, in the Slovak National Party, in addition to confronting the communist party. The more rapid pluralization of Slovak political forces promoted a rather more coherent self-definition and effective organization in PAV than has occurred in the CF, which has as yet no major non-communist opponent in the Czech Republic. At its September 1990 congress, PAV elected a new leadership and adopted new statutes, which included a definition of six 'basic programmatic goals', formal membership requirements and rights, and a clarification of its internal structure.[23]

PAV's programmatic orientation has been shaped by the demands of the Slovak political environment. The leading figures in the foundation of PAV included scientists, doctors, and other intellectuals, who first became engaged in oppositional activities in the Bratislava environmental movement in the 1980s. It thus had at the start a pronounced 'green' tinge, but the Slovak national question has quickly gained priority in the Slovak political agenda. PAV has developed an identity as the defender of Slovak interests within the framework of a radically reformed federal framework, contrasting with the more or less overt separatism of the Christian Democratic Movement and the nationalists.

PAV leaders' vigorous defence of Slovak autonomy has brought conflicts with the CF, but PAV shares the basic liberal-democratic and pro-market values central to its Czech sister movement. In the Slovak context, these have a distinctive appeal to specific social groups and regions as a secular, more 'modern', or Western-oriented, alternative to the Christian traditionalism and aggressive Slovak nationalism of its main rivals, and thus are the basis for the future gradual development of the movement towards a party form.

The CF's dominant position in the as yet barely formed political spectrum in the Czech Republic reflects the rather greater degree of homogeneity of Czech society. Urban-rural and religious cleavages are less pronounced, while the reviving, but still weak, sense of Czech national identity is closely bound up with Masarykian ethical-humanistic liberalism, which transcends political-ideological divisions and has a universalistic appeal.[24] Correspondingly, the aim to represent the *whole* society is quite deeply embedded in the movement's philosophy, as well as reflecting the absence in reality of powerful competitors. As a CF election leaflet explained: 'In contrast to most of the other 21 political parties, movements and coalitions [registered for the election], which often only pursue the claims of partial interests of particular groups of the population, Civic Forum basically takes account of the interests of all citizens.'[25] The characteristic election slogan was 'Parties are for party members – Civic Forum is for everyone'. The role of the CF was thus originally seen as quite different from that of a political party, as more of a forum for supra-political, educative, participatory experience. One activist described its role as being to 'remove from our people apathy, passivity, formalism, dissimulation, fear and other deformations of public life'.[26] A draft programme in early 1990 described the CF as 'a democratic civic force, protecting autonomous groups from possible attempts by the state to coopt them'. Havel in particular hoped that the CF would draw into politics individual citizens untrammelled by political ideologies.[27]

There was from the start considerable uncertainty among the leaders of the movements about the implications of this approach: on the one hand, it was recognized that this amorphousness was the source of its appeal to a public that had a 'real antipathy to joining anything' and a suspicion of party discipline and bureaucracy; on the other, the claim to universalism was seen as a potential danger, undermining legitimate opponents and exposing the movement to the temptation of creating 'another closed system' in which it could 'exercise absolute power and

61

make the same mistakes the communists did'.[28] The CF quickly came under fire from both outside and inside: it was accused on the one hand of fostering a 'new totalitarianism', and on the other of being weakly organized and deficient in central control over local branches and central accountability to the local level.

These apparently contradictory accusations had some basis in practice. Because there was no formal membership, there were no rules for admission. This exposed the movement to the danger of infiltration by opportunist former communists anxious to retain their positions. Local groups on occasion fell into bitter internal wrangles on this issue, in which the central leaders found it difficult to intervene. A particularly vicious public dispute in the Brno group between some radically anti-communist 'angry young men' and the supporters of an ex-communist veteran Charter 77 activist lost the movement much public credibility prior to the June elections, and helped the rise of an alternative region-alist challenge from a body calling itself Movement for Self-Governing Democracy, which promoted claims for Moravian and Silesian autonomy. Moreover, the role of the CF groups in enterprises was controversial, especially when they took on responsibility for determining what was to happen to communist-appointed enterprise managers. Everywhere, as communist power rapidly disintegrated, the CF was drawn into the role of nominating candidates for vacant posts and of vetting new appointments, which exposed them to the accusation of reviving the *nomenklatura* system. And without adequate structures of accountability and generally accepted fair rules for the assessment of former communists, this new power could easily be abused, and used for settling local personal scores, thereby threatening to disrupt the functioning of the economy and the state administration.[29] Divisions between the local activists and the CF's national leaders have also emerged on this question, some local associations being markedly more radical on the question of removing local *nomenklatura* officials than the centre.[30]

At the centre in Prague, the emergency cooptation of leading CF personalities into government positions deprived the movement of experienced officials with established personal authority, which hindered organizational development. The central Coordinating Committee of the CF was increasingly absorbed in 'high politics', and was attacked for becoming 'an autonomous group of political negotiators eluding supervision, taking decisions in the name of society', and looking increasingly like the apparat of a political party but lacking intermediary links with the still amorphous grass-roots movement, which continued to go its own way.[31]

In October 1990, the CF's Republican Assembly met to approve a modest formalization of the movement's structure, but a large majority were against turning it into a political party. Commitment to 'horizontality' was reaffirmed, and membership remained informal, in contrast to PAV, which had decided to register its members. Local groups were supposed to 'record' (*evidovat*) participants in the movement, but some remained resistant even to this as excessively 'party-like'.[32] During the autumn of 1990, however, the mood in the movement shifted markedly towards accepting the necessity of tighter organizational structures to combat a sense of leadership drift and the lack of communication between the movement's governmental and parliamentary representatives and its grass-roots supporters. The election of Vaclav Klaus, the Federal Minister of Finance, to the new post of the CF Chairman (against Havel's preferred candidate Martin Palous) signalled this change of mood. It also brought to a head both strategic and programmatic questions. Klaus has wide popularity and visibility in Czechoslovak politics, or, more accurately, in the Czech Republic, as a decisive and energetic proponent of radical and rapid economic transformation; but he is also a divisive figure, on account of both his somewhat abrasive personality and his strong commitment to neo-liberal economics and right-of-centre political values. At the same time, the formation of an 'Interparliamentary Club of the Democratic Right', which rapidly gathered the allegiance of a substantial number of CF deputies, appeared to show gathering momentum for a distinct ideological shift to the right of the CF as a whole. However, these developments on the right of the movement called forth a reaction not only from the left but also from the centrist progessive liberals. The left formed an 'Inter-Parliamentary Civic Association' among CF deputies, and a 'Liberal Club' also formed around some of the former leading 'dissidents' of Charter 77 who have prominent positions in the government.

In January 1991, the CF's Republican Assembly took further steps towards reforming the movement as a political party, which included the adoption of a set of programmatic principles and further reorganization. A major shift towards clearer ideological self-definition was marked by a formal rejection in the programme of 'socialist ideologies of any type'. Thus the minority leftist faction has been effectively forced out. A new Executive Committee was set up comprising seventeen members, under the chairmanship of Vaclav Klaus, which includes ten seats for regional representatives and three seats each for representatives of the two parliamentary factions, the Inter-Parliamentary Club of the Democratic Right and the Liberal Club. These two factions became more formalized after a further CF Congress on 23 February, at which the right wing constituted itself as the 'Civic Democratic Party', and the liberal centre formed a more loosely organized 'Civic Movement'. Both have agreed in the meanwhile to work together in parliament under the common CF banner, and to refrain from attempting to take over the CF; but they are likely to be propelled further into conflict and competition as the next general election, due in 1992, approaches.

The dilemmas that Solidarity and the CF have confronted in the post-communist period have been largely absent from Hungarian politics. This is primarily due to the particular, gradualistic pattern of breakdown of communist rule in Hungary. By the time of the March-April 1990 general election, the various movements and parties had had more than two years of remarkable freedom in which to develop their organization and identity. After the collapse of the HSWP in October 1989, in fact, the two major non-communist political forces that had emerged – the Hungarian Democratic Forum (HDF) and the Alliance of Free Democrats (AFD) – had the 'luxury' of campaigning as much against each other as against the communists. Although both started out as movement-parties, more or less consciously following the Solidarity model, they have progressed much further in the direction of the party form. Their main task now is not so much self-definition as developing their membership-base and their grass-roots organization, since, unlike Solidarity, the CF or PAV, they were launched 'from above' on the initiative of elite, intelligentsia-dominated groups, rather than being propelled into life by a mass social movement.

The HDF was originally founded as a 'non-political movement' in September 1987 by a section of the cultural intelligentsia associated with populist-nationalist views. In fact, many of its early adherents were not 'dissident' opposition activists, but dissaffected members of the cultural establishment, which goes some way to explaining their consistently cooperative, non-confrontational approach to the communist authorities. At first, the stated aim was to act as a loose-knit club for the discussion of the state of the nation and the ways out of the crisis; a little later, the role of 'bridge between the state and society' was proposed, but the aim, it was emphasized, was not to challenge the HSWP's 'leading role'. Although this accommodating stance did not save them from attack by Kadar and other conservative HSWP leaders in 1987 and early 1988, Imre Pozsgay, the leader of HSWP's growing reformist wing, offered his support to the movement, which he saw as a potential partner for the party.[33] In his view, the HSWP needed to broaden its popular credibility by conducting dialogue with representatives of society, and, for Pozsgay, the Christian, nationalist and populist intelligentsia were more congenial interlocutors than the more radical committed 'dissident' activists in the Democratic Opposition. The HDF in turn was willing to work with the communist regime insofar as it promoted political reform and dialogue. Securing gradual and peaceful change, compromise and accommodation with the existing authorities and avoiding social upheaval therefore became from the start embedded in its approach and, by the time of the 1990 elections, were reflected in its economic programme, which rejected 'shock therapy' and emphasized gradualism and stability. Although electioneering in competition with the AFD required the adoption of more overtly anti-communist rhetoric to ward off the charge of being soft on communism, the HDF nevertheless appears to have drawn at least part of its support from communists who were fearful of political reprisals should the more radical parties win the elections.

The HDF underwent the process of self-questioning now absorbing Solidarity and the CF some time before standing for election. At first, in 1988, there was considerable resistance within the original leading group, dominated by populists, to forming a political party. It was objected that the aim of the HDF was to represent 'society as a whole', to unify rather than divide, and more such familiar concepts. But in the rapidly pluralizing political environment of 1989, when parties were legalized and free elections were agreed, the supra-political interpretation of the HDF's role gave way to the development of a more party-like form. Moreover, the membership of the movement expanded rapidly, drawing in a wider spectrum of opinion. The populist-nationalist tendency has thus given way to more moderate liberal nationalists, Christians and traditionalist conservatives. The development of the Forum into a West European type of Christian Democratic party is the avowed aim of Jozsef Antall, who was elected leader in 1989; under Antall, the HDF has not only been accepted into the Christian Democrat International, but played host to that association's conference in Budapest in 1990. The Forum has picked up local support among professionals and the middle classes in provincial towns, but its penetration to the smaller localities remains weak, as evidenced by the September 1990 local elections, in which independents were far more successful than candidates for any of the main parties.

The HDF's main opponent, the AFD, originated in early 1988 as a coalitional movement under the name 'Network of Free Initiatives', acting as a coordinating centre for a variety of independent oppositional groups. The nucleus was the hard core of the Democratic Opposition of dissident intellectuals, most of whom lived in Budapest but who were also present in provincial university towns, who had been active in *samizdat* publishing and human-rights issues since the late 1970s. The AFD also gathered the support of a number of leading economists and social scientists (thus contrasting in intellectual flavour with the historians and poets who were central to the founding of the HDF), many of whom had been closely involved with the Hungarian government in drawing up economic reform proposals. These defected to the opposition in the mid-1980s, having lost all hope of seeing a consistent economic reform implemented as long as the HSWP retained its political monopoly. The AFD has thus come to stand for radical and rapid economic transformation. It emphasizes secular and liberal political values, and advocates universal human rights rather than nationalism. Like the Democratic Union and ROAD in Poland, it espouses a clear 'Western' identity, rejecting a special Hungarian 'third way' first espoused by interwar populists and revived by some sections of the HDF. But, unlike ROAD in Poland, which has upheld the compromise with the old regime made in 1989, the AFD has adopted a radical anti-communist stance, advocating a clean break with the past and exhibiting militant hostility towards the HSWP/HSP and towards Pozsgay personally.

The AFD was, until autumn 1989, much less widely known than the HDF, which had gained prominence in organizing public demonstrations in support of Hungarian minority-rights in Transylvania and had received coverage in the section of the Hungarian media controlled by the Patriotic People's Front, which Pozsgay chaired. Both movements were members of the Opposition Round Table that coordinated opposition forces in the summer 1989 negotiations with the HSWP, but a split between them developed over the issue of the Presidency (for which Pozsgay would have been the strongest candidate). The AFD successfully petitioned for a referendum on the issue, and then won public support, by a slim majority, for direct election of the Presidency, which they preferred. They thus won public visibility and self-confidence, whereas the HDF mishandled the referendum by unsuccessfully urging a boycott of it. The AFD's membership thereafter grew rapidly. In the March election campaign, it appeared to be running neck-to-neck with the HDF, but it performed rather less well in the first round of the elections, particularly in Budapest, which had been assumed to be natural AFD territory, having a high concentration of educated, secular-oriented voters. In the second round, it managed to retain the loyalty of its voters, but the HDF gained disproportionately by the transfer of votes to it from supporters of parties that were eliminated or performed weakly in the first round. Thus the AFD ended up in parliament as the main opposition party, but with a substantially smaller representation than the HDF (see Appendix). The continuing volatility of voter support for all parties was indicated by the AFD's remarkable come-back in Budapest in the subsequent local elections; but like the HDF, its penetration to the localities outside Budapest remains weak.

The AFD has a partner – and potential challenger – in the Alliance of Young Democrats (Fidesz), which is a unique phenomenon in East Central Europe. It has never been the 'youth wing' of the AFD, although it espouses essentially the same values. It arose independently in 1988 among Budapest students, many of whom were enrolled in the law faculty of the university. The two groups represent an important generational divide within the Hungarian radical-liberal intelligentsia, based on very different formative experiences. The AFD's core group started out their political careers in student movements of the late 1960s and early 1970s, and have since suffered years of police harassment and intimidation in rather isolated circumstances. To some extent, life in the underground has left its mark on their somewhat clannish political style. Fidesz, by contrast, comprises a generation of young people who came of age in the last decade of declining Kadarism. They exhibit a freshness, openness and sense of humour that has proved very attractive to voters of all ages, their youthfulness itself being seen as a guarantee of the real break with the past. They have been able to distance themselves from the more sterile political wrangling between the HDF and the AFD, and the performance of their leading representatives in parliament has earned them wide respect for sharpness, competence and coherence.

Let us now turn briefly to some of the other political forces that the movement-parties face as either competitors or coalition partners. First of all, we should note the divergent paths of the East-Central European communist parties. In both Poland and Hungary, the communist parties have undergone profound crises, having split and renamed themselves. The first to go was the HSWP, which effectively dissolved itself at its Extraordinary Congress in October 1989 to form a Hungarian Socialist Party espousing Western-style social-democratic values, to which former HSWP members were invited to apply. This was proved to have been a major tactical blunder on the part of the leadership under Rezso Nyers, when only 10,000 of the over 700,000 former HSWP members applied to join in the first month; strenuous recruitment efforts over the following months brought the membership to around 50,000. This made the HSP appear at the time a relatively strong political force by comparison with other parties and movements, but its credibility with voters, who were now offered a free choice, had been badly damaged. They also lost ground as overt anti-communist sentiments, which had been rather muted in Hungary, became more popular in the autumn of 1989 as a response to the dramatic events in the region, and especially in Romania.

In the meanwhile, the hardline conservative core of the old HSWP regrouped and started an embarrassing wrangle with the HSP for control of the assets of the former HSWP. The HSWP failed to clear the 4 per cent barrier in the general election and was thus relegated to a marginal position in Hungarian politics. The HSP, by contrast, playing on the high political profiles of its leading reformists, such as Imre Pozsgay and Gyula Horn, and still enjoying the benefits of former HSWP facilities, recovered to some extent in the elections to become the fourth largest party in parliament on the basis of about 11 per cent of the vote. But the loss of Imre Pozsgay, who resigned his membership in November 1990 and is still searching for a suitable role in Hungarian politics, has been a further blow to their popular standing.[34]

The PUWP decided to dissolve itself at the end of 1989, and the factionalism that had always been characteristic of it gave way to disintegration. Two new parties emerged from the rubble, the major one, the Social Democracy of the Republic of Poland, claiming the right to inherit the PUWP's assets. A smaller faction, led by Tadcusz Fischbach, the reformist PUWP secretary in Gdansk in 1980–81, calls itself the Social Democratic Union of the Polish Republic and strives to represent a more clear-cut break with the past than its larger rival. Both parties, however, appear to have virtually no electoral appeal.[35]

The situation in Czechoslovakia is quite different: the communist party has not renamed itself (although a few voices have been raised supporting this). It has, however, undergone internal federalization, which has created separate parties in Bohemia and Moravia, and in Slovakia. It has lost large numbers of members, but still claims 750,000 on its records, although most of these are probably passive and will eventually drop out altogether.[36] Nevertheless, it has proved remarkably resilient in its electoral performance, winning 15–20 per cent of the vote (see Appendix). This suggests that it may still be able to muster votes from groups feeling threatened by the economic reform, in addition to the loyal former *aparatnici* who probably form its core electoral support. It has the advantage in addition of a minimally disrupted country-wide organizational structure and access to assets that the new Federal Assembly decided to confiscate only in November 1990.

In general, the parties of the non-communist left (the Social Democrats in Hungary and Czechoslovakia, and the Polish Socialist Party, as well as the Czechoslovak Socialist Party, which was a former partner of the Communist Party in the 'National Front') have been far less successful than either outside observers or they themselves expected. There are common reasons for this: the 'historical' parties, revived from the pre-communist period, are bedevilled by bitter conflicts between the older generation of leaders, traceable to the fraught past histories of the parties and personalities involved; and between the older generation and the younger generation of new members, many of whom were until recently communist party members, but who now espouse a modern variant of social democracy quite at odds with the older generation's more Marxist concepts. There are tensions between those who have returned from decades in emigration, those who stayed at home and were imprisoned, and those who compromised with the communist party. The potential for splintering into rival fragments is obvious, and, where this has happened, it has only further damaged their electoral chances in an already unpropitious political environment for socialists. Their space on the ideological spectrum as 'democratic socialists' has, moreover, been appropriated by the reformed communist parties.

Personality conflicts and undignified fights over the historical heritage seem to have been a problem common to many of the so-called 'historical' parties of all shades of opinion. The more traditionalist parties, which may receive strong support from émigré communities, also have to confront tendencies to nostalgia that appear to have little appeal to the new electorate. One of the more successful 'historical' parties so far has been the Independent Smallholders Party in Hungary, which is a revival of the party reformed in 1945, and which successfully mobilized the anti-communist vote in the 1945 and 1947 elections. It has now won a place as the HDF's key partner in the Antall government coalition, but has a narrow, regional electoral base and has created enormous problems by insisting on the implementation of its key electoral promise to return all farmland to its 1947 owners or their descendants (see Chapter 4).

An even more successful party resting on 'historical' foundations is the Christian Democratic Movement (CDM) of Slovakia, led by Jan Carnogursky with the support of his brother Ivan. These men come from something of a Bratislava political dynasty, their father having been a prominent figure in the interwar Slovak People's Party. Despite the adoption of the Christian Democratic name, this party has some way to go if it is to conform to the West European concept of Christian Democracy, and, at present, the leadership does not appear to be able or willing to move too fast in this direction. It is profoundly traditionalist and overwhelmingly Catholic in orientation. It is also nationalist and separatist, although it differentiates itself from the proto-fascist Slovak National Party by adopting a more 'realistic' or vaguely defined timeframe for the transition to full independence for Slovakia.[37] The CDM is a difficult junior partner for the PAV-dominated governing coalition in Slovakia, and will play a pivotal role in the future of the federation itself. On the one hand, it could easily overtake PAV in electoral support, which would probably lead to renewed demands for increased Slovak autonomy and raise the possibility of protracted constitutional crisis. On the other hand, the CDM has the ability to draw voters away from the more extreme variants of Slovak nationalism (rather in the way in which the Bavarian CSU was able to draw support away from neo-Nazi movements in West Germany under Franz Jozef Strauss). To that extent, it may serve to preserve democracy in Slovakia, without which the federation is certainly doomed.

In Poland, the proliferation of new parties outside Solidarity has proceeded unchecked as yet by the pressures for coalescence, which will come only when the first free general-election campaign begins in the spring of 1991. The Presidential election already saw the beginnings of a coalescence of forces – not only within Solidarity but also from outside it – around the person of Lech Walesa: the Centre Accord proved able to call on support from a range of Christian, national and peasant parties from which in the future a right-of-centre coalition might be forged. The peasant parties – at present very much at odds with each other – have the potential in the longer term to form a distinctive grouping with not only a history and a place in the political traditions of Poland, but also a large and vocal (if far from homogeneous) social constituency in the Polish peasantry.[38]

For all the confusion and instability of emergent political pluralism in East Central Europe at the beginning of 1991, certain positive trends of development can already be detected. Although the internal conflicts of the movement-parties seem bewildering and even disillusioning to many of their members, the process of pluralization has to be accepted as an inevitable phase in the transition to democracy, without which the real diversity of interests in the respective societies cannot find legitimate channels of expression. There may be bitter arguments about whether such pluralization is premature in the given situation, where there are strong arguments for maintaining unity in order to carry the society through the traumatic period of economic transformation, but there is also a case to be made for pluralization in order to sustain the credibility of parliaments as open representative institutions, and to ensure the continuing responsiveness of governments to the full spectrum of opinion. Democracy in East Central Europe will be forged in the baptism of fire of economic transformation, to which we turn in the following chapter.

4

THE POLITICS OF ECONOMIC TRANSFORMATION

All past attempts at economic reform in East Central Europe failed primarily because of the political obstacles posed by the communist parties' monopoly of political power. The ideology of the regimes placed severe constraints on the elaboration of models of economic reform by insisting that central control over economic processes be retained to an extent that undermined the effectiveness of the operation of markets. Even where, as in Hungary and Poland, party leaders were prepared to sacrifice important elements of the ideology for the sake of coherence in the economic reform, they found it impossible to put the reform into practice because of the resistance of bureaucratic interests entrenched in the power structures upon which their own positions ultimately depended. Moreover, the regimes lacked basic popular legitimacy, and thus faced an unacceptable risk of mass revolt in reaction to the inevitable impact of economic reform on the standard of living, particularly that of workers in hitherto high-priority traditional industrial sectors.

The events of 1989 have fundamentally changed these political conditions by sweeping away the power of the communist parties and their ideology: the economic task is thus no longer 'reform' but 'transformation', or, as Miklos Nemeth (the last Hungarian communist Prime Minister) put it, the creation of 'a market economy without any qualifying adjectives'. The stated aim of the new regimes is to 'separate economics from politics': that is, to bring about an economic system that can function primarily according to the laws of the market rather than according to bureaucratic political preferences imposed, often against all economic logic, through directive central planning. Government intervention in the

72

economy thus should undergo a qualitative change, to become guided by, rather than overriding, these laws; it will, moreover, be subjected to free public criticism and checked by democratic parliamentary control.

Nevertheless, economics will remain profoundly political, not only because this is the case in every politico-economic system, but because in the specific context of East Central Europe the task of economic transformation presents unprecedented political challenges. Democracy may be a necessary political condition, but it is by no means sufficient to guarantee a trouble-free and popularly supported passage to a market economy, especially given the profoundly disturbed state of the economies of East Central Europe; and, as we already began to see in Chapter 3, their democracies are still based on fragile foundations. There are apparently convincing political arguments for gradualism in the economic transition; democracy itself would suffer if untested and over-hasty radical economic measures provoked mass popular rejection of the new governments. But there are also convincing arguments for 'shock therapy' – rapid and simultaneous introduction of the basic requisites of a market economy – on both political and economic grounds. It is not clear that economic gradualism under democratic rule would be more successful than it was under reform communist rule, or that gradualism can realistically promise to soften the economic blow. 'Shock therapy' could shorten the painful period of transition, but at the risk of intensifying its social and political impact. But the fact that the task of economic transformation is quite unprecedented means that both lines of argument rest on unproven assumptions, and therefore that it will inevitably remain a subject of intense debate among economic experts, which in turn will breed doubt and scepticism in society and generate conflict among politicians. But doubts must be overcome, and conflicts managed and resolved, if anything is to be achieved. What is required is clearly 'strong' government, but in a form that is also compatible with the preservation and development of democracy – a tall order indeed.

Ralf Dahrendorf, reflecting on the relevance of the experience of West Germany in the immediate postwar period for East Central Europe today, has pointed to the 'incompatible time-scales of political and economic reform'.[1] Whereas political change can be effected in a matter of months, economic recovery takes several years; in the intervening period, the passage through the 'valley of tears' of economic upheaval and social dislocation makes extraordinary demands on political leadership. A major ingredient of the West German success, according to Dahrendorf, was the particular constellation of personalities of that time:

on the one hand, there was an economic team led by Ludwig Erhard, with a clear-headed and determined commitment to economic liberalism, presented in a package labelled the 'social market economy'; on the other, there was the Chancellor, Konrad Adenauer, whose personal authority provided the 'political cover' for the programme; and, finally, there was a group of politicians, notably Thomas Blank, first Federal Minister of Social Affairs, Hans Katzer, chairman of the CDU 'Employees' Committee', and the trade-union leader Hans Bockler, whose contribution was to make the social guarantees effective:

> The conclusion is that it takes more than one political leader to achieve this feat. Somebody has to provide the protection of political power, somebody has to have the practical courage to take an economy from central planning to more open pastures, and somebody has to insist on certain social policies which are appropriate in their own right and also make the harsher side effects of the new-found market bearable.[2]

In this chapter, we begin with a general outline of the dimensions of economic transformation, in order to clarify the nature of the political challenge it poses. In the second section, we will examine the new governments' preparedness to meet this challenge in terms of their internal cohesiveness, their parliamentary support-base, and the extent of their popular legitimacy. We will also focus on particular political 'flashpoints' in the early stages of economic transformation in order to illustrate the emerging new patterns of interaction between politics and economics.

From economic reform to economic transformation

The attempts at economic reform under communist rule in East Central Europe until the 1980s were based on a model of what has been called 'the regulated market' system, and assumed the continuation of state ownership of the major part of land and productive assets.[3] The failure of this approach to generate any significant improvement in economic performance led to its complete rejection by economists in East Central Europe, and its more or less explicit abandonment by the communist regimes in Poland and Hungary in the 1980s. The aim of this model was to improve efficiency, not by abandoning planning altogether, but by changing its focus significantly, in order to allow substantial enterprise autonomy and the revival of the role of the market at the microeconomic level. The central planners and industrial branch ministries would no longer be concerned with drawing up detailed annual plan-targets for enterprises, but would concentrate on the medium- and longer-range perspectives of development of the economy as a whole, of geographical regions and selected priority branches. Enterprises would draw up their own production and development plans on the basis of market stimuli, and would have the right to choose their suppliers, set their own prices, and offer performance-related incentives and bonuses to their employees. But planners would continue to exert considerable control over enterprises *indirectly* in order to ensure that the basic economic trends developed in conformity with central objectives, or, as the model's proponents put it, in conformity with 'the social interest'. The central authorities retained control over the use of enterprise assets and the distribution of their income by means of 'regulators': i.e. rules governing deductions to the state budget, wage-setting and bonuses, the retention of funds for decentralized investment, and so on. The major part of resources for investment remained under the control of the central authorities, and far-reaching price and wage policies were also employed.

Even in theory, it was clear that the market and enterprise autonomy were going to be very much more circumscribed than in the case of even the most developed corporatist, welfare-state variant of Western capitalism; in practice, the model turned out to be little more than a modified version of central planning. Even where the model prescribed scope for autonomous enterprise decision-making, managers usually found it easier, if not essential, to rely on informal contacts with the central authorities, and because the ministries still controlled the appointment and promotion of enterprise managers, the latter had strong reasons to comply with informal central demands, even where these might conflict with the economic interests of the enterprise. Access to centralized investment, subsidies to continue import-substituting production, negotiations around wage regulations and price-setting all still required constant close interaction between planners, ministerial bureaucrats and managers. Moreover, no satisfactory provision for bankruptcy of economically unviable enterprises was made in the reform. The 'plan bargaining' that had characterized the traditional system was therefore merely replaced by bargaining over the regulators;[4] enterprises thus achieved not autonomy but at best 'dual dependence', vertically on the bureaucracy and horizontally on their customers and suppliers.[5] The system in Hungary was described by one of its foremost critics as one of 'neither plan nor market',[6] pointing up not only the internal contra-dictions of the model but also the state of imminent paralysis to which it was leading in practice.

But what also became clear in the course of the reforms was the crucial role played by political obstacles to radical change in the economy: the interlocking interests of managers and state bureaucrats in minimizing the operation of the market and undermining enterprise autonomy and managerial responsibility. This came to be seen as the central problem of the economic reform model itself. As we have seen in Chapter 1, these interlocking bureaucratic interests were closely tied into the structure of communist party power itself. A solution to the economic problem thus required the end to the communist party's monopoly of power; but it also required the establishment of firmer economic foundations for enterprise autonomy. Even before the disintegration of communist power, the regimes of Poland and Hungary took some steps in this direction by, for example, abolishing the meddlesome industrial branch ministries, breaking up the giant monopolistic enterprises, introducing forms of enterprise self-management councils with responsibility for managerial appointment, and expanding the scope for certain types of small-scale private enterprise. But, by the 1980s, East Central Europe's economists were convinced that the crucial ingredient of the transformation of decaying state corporatist economies into dynamic, flexible market economies was missing. That ingredient was the wholesale privatization of the bulk of productive assets, an objective that came onto the public agenda only after the removal of the communist parties from power.

Privatization as a general objective appears to have won majority support not only among economic experts but also among the new political elites and the populations as a whole. Although there may still be some room for academic debate about the necessity of private ownership for the effective operation of a market economy,[7] practical experience has convinced East-Central Europeans that the two cannot be separated. As a result, there is now deep reluctance to entertain any further experiments in search of alternative 'third roads' between capitalism and socialism, and a preference for policies and programmes that have been tried and found to work at least reasonably well in West European countries. Thus privatization is accepted as a component of the broad political programme of the 'return to Europe'.

However, the initial sympathetic reception of the idea of privatization in general has rapidly given way to acute controversy and conflict within the new governments, parliaments and public opinion about how to proceed. The establishment of new firms on the basis of private capital from domestic or foreign sources is generally welcomed, but the question of transferring existing state enterprises to private ownership poses much greater economic and political problems. For one thing, there is the technical complexity of the task in itself, and the lack of precedents for privatization on such a scale. For another, as concrete plans for privatization of specific enterprises are drawn up, so the initial socio-political consensus gives way to sharp differentiation, if not polarization, of attitudes. Privatization raises not just technical economic questions, but political questions (narrowly defined) of winners and losers, and (broadly defined) of social justice.

Thus, although a broad consensus can be reached on the desirability of privatization *per se*, serious economic and political dilemmas begin to develop when the question of implementation comes to be considered.[8] Three possible courses have been identified in the East-Central European debates: restitution to former owners, sale to new private owners, or free distribution of shares to the population as a whole. The reasoning behind the restitution argument is mainly ethical: confiscated property ought to be returned to its rightful owners. It is thus connected with the political legitimation of the new regimes, which are expected by the people to rectify the wrongs committed under communist rule, and generally to show respect for property rights. However, in practice, restitution will be a far from straightforward matter: there is the problem of identifying the original owners, whose legal title to property may be hard to establish, who may have emigrated or died in the meanwhile. The legal owners or their heirs either may not know of their rights to regain their property, or may no longer be interested in it. Moreover, in many cases, the property will have undergone change in the course of time, either degenerating through neglect, or being transformed and extended by investment in the past decades under state control. The property in these cases cannot simply be returned to former owners; but the impoverished and indebted states cannot offer to provide satisfactory financial compensation for losses or to buy out the shares of former private owners. What they can offer in the form of shares or bonds may not be seen as adequate by the former owners. Legislation on restitution must therefore allow a reasonable time for people to submit their claims, and for these to be authenticated and adjudicated fairly. This necessarily prolongs the period of uncertainty about the status of all property, delaying the process of privatization in general and creating considerable uncertainty, which discourages urgently needed new investment, particularly of foreign capital. In Hungary, where the restitution of agricultural land to former private owners has been a subject of bitter controversy, this uncertainty is threatening to disrupt agricultural production, and thus not only domestic food supplies but export earnings. Restitution is likely to have a further undesirable effect, in addition to delaying economic transformation, in that it perpetuates the tendency of people to direct their energies into claiming resources from the state rather than to work hard to earn such resources.

As for the second option – the transfer of state property into new private hands – the most straightforward approach would appear to be outright sale to the highest bidder at auctions. The advantage of this is clearly that it would provide revenue to overstretched state budgets. Moreover, property would presumably end up in the hands of those most interested in using it to best economic effect. But how to establish a fair price, in the absence of functioning capital markets? And to whom to sell? A major problem is the inadequacy of domestic sources of capital, but it is politically unacceptable to allow free rein to foreign capital, which would undermine the government's legitimacy as defender of the national interest, especially where there are no means of determining an objectively fair price, thus exposing it to charges of simply 'selling out' national assets at knock-down prices to foreigners. Moreover, there is the question of enterprise debts: will the new owners also take these over, or can the state afford simply to write them off?

Selling state property to the highest bidder unavoidably favours the rich, which would be controversial anywhere, but even more so in the East European context, where the rich tend to be members of the former *nomenklatura*, who turn out again to be the winners even in the new post-communist conditions, transforming their political power into economic power – to the understandable rage of the rest of society. Banks might be able to offer credits to broaden access to ownership, but such credits would have to be tightly controlled in order to prevent their feeding additional inflationary pressures into the economy, and they would present high risks, since banks would have no way of assessing the entrepreneurial record of the new owners.

Moreover, the earlier reforms introducing enterprise self-management councils have also created ambiguities about property rights: does the state still 'own' self-managed firms, or have property rights been transferred to employees? In Hungary and Czechoslovakia, the new governments have had to 'renationalize' enterprises, while in Poland a powerful 'self-management' lobby in parliament has created considerable obstacles to the passage of privatization law. If the workers are to be bought out, how much compensation for the loss of their property rights should they be offered, and will they accept this in principle? Should workers be permitted priority rights in the purchase of shares at special, reduced prices? Workers in profitable and viable enterprises would do much better than workers in neglected and underinvested enterprises, and their relative positions could hardly be related to their respective merits as workers. But why should enterprise workers be so privileged at all? What about the interests of non-workers or the retired? After all, as Kornai points out: 'The wealth embodied by the firm at the moment of ownership transfer has not been created exclusively by that firm's workers; every citizen has contributed through the state investments and the state subsidies the firm has received.'[9]

Finally, of course, we must not lose sight of the fundamental *economic* purpose of privatization. In Kornai's view, 'the prime consideration is not legal entitlement to acquire property but the ability to run it well'.[10] It is not clear, to say the least, that full self-management will bring such efficiency with it.

A further major drawback of privatization through direct sales is the time it would take to make real inroads into the massive state sector. In Britain, the privatization of a few state firms has taken ten years; at the equivalent pace in Hungary, it would take a century to reduce state ownership to proportions comparable with those found in Western economies. For Kornai, the conclusion is that an extended period of 'dual economy' must be reckoned with, since in his view 'it is impossible to institute private property by cavalry attack'.[11] But if, as other East European economists are convinced, private property is a necessary concomitant of the establishment of the market, a quicker solution must be found.

This concern lies behind the third scheme for privatization: the free distribution of shares to the population at large. This would be done by providing all adults with vouchers, which they could then exchange for shares in companies of their choice. Competitive bidding by prospective share purchasers would thus help generate market 'prices' for shares, which could then be used as a basis for direct sales to foreign and domestic purchasers. This scheme appears to have the further merit of social justice, since it is in accord with the assumption that all citizens have an equal interest in state property. But it is an untried, and therefore highly risky, approach. It is likely to prove very costly to administer, and will not generate revenue for the state budget. Moreover, in the case of heavily indebted states, there could be argued to be prior claims on the part of foreign creditors to some share in the state's assets. It could also be argued that it would be a dereliction of duty on the part of the state simply to give away national assets to all and sundry: 'Its apparatus is obliged to handle the wealth it was entrusted with carefully until a new owner appears who can guarantee a safer and more efficient guardianship.'[12]

The free distribution of shares would create a wide dispersal of ownership among inexperienced and possibly indifferent shareholders, and would thus be unlikely to produce the effective check on managerial performance that is supposed to be the main result of privatization. To some extent this problem could be expected to diminish over time as shareholding became concentrated in fewer hands. From the public's point of view, even disregarding its lack of experience, the difficulty of assessing the relative merits of companies would be enormous, given the lack of objective market information to start with.

It is thus not surprising that privatization legislation has taken longer to materialize than originally expected. In Hungary and Poland, some backtracking occurred in 1990, as the state sought to regain control over the process after some highly unpopular and politically damaging scandals that arose as a result of 'wild' privatizations in which state assets were acquired by enterprise managers and former *nomenklatura* officials without proper valuation or outside control. Corruption seems to be an endemic risk in the process. Nevertheless, by the end of 1990, all three countries in our study had prepared more or less detailed privatization plans.

In Hungary, both restitution and the voucher scheme have been rejected in favour of direct sales, and accordingly the government at first seemed committed to a rather slower pace than in Poland and Czechoslovakia. In terms of preparation, however, Hungary is further advanced than its neighbours, having begun to implement the necessary legislation to transform state enterprises into joint-stock companies from the beginning of 1989.[13] A series of state enterprises were put up for sale in the last months of 1990, after some hesitation and delay, but the State Property Agency (SPA), which has been set up to oversee the process, also turned down a number of proposals.[14] A major stumbling-block in Hungary has proved to be the question of reprivatization of agricultural land, which has divided the government coalition and been rejected by the High Court as unconstitutional. The question has diverted attention from the overall strategy of privatization, into which it must be integrated consistently. Following government changes at the end of 1990, a more accelerated pace seems likely. In January 1991, new regulations were introduced permitting interested investors to initiate privatization by making an offer to the SPA. A wider range of employee and management buy-out schemes is also in preparation. Over three to five years, the government expects to privatize 50–60 per cent of state assets.

In Poland, more than a dozen drafts of privatization legislation were considered by the Sejm between autumn 1989 and July 1990, when a compromise was reached. A major point of conflict emerged between, on the one hand, representatives of workers in the large state enterprises (Solidarity's traditional bedrock of support), and allied proponents of self-management, who argued forcefully for transfer of ownership to enterprise employees, and, on the other, the government, backed by the majority of Solidarity deputies, whose proposals aimed at unrestricted sales and distribution by vouchers. Considerable popular hostility emerged to the sale of state property to foreigners. The Act on Privatization that resulted from these cross-pressures has been described as 'eclectic', and to some extent has merely postponed final decisions about actual privatization.[15] But it provides a flexible framework, allowing for a wide variety of methods of privatization, including the sale of shares, the use of vouchers, and some preferential allocations of up to 20 per cent of enterprise shares to employees. Foreign investors can buy up to 10 per cent of any enterprise's shares, but beyond that, approval must be won from the president of the Foreign Investment Agency. This restriction was greeted with dismay by potential Western investors, but the government has attempted to reassure them that such approval was likely to be granted readily. The current expectation is that about 50 per cent of state enterprises should be privatized within three years.

In Czechoslovakia, a Restitution Law has been a matter of lengthy debate. The original draft, published in autumn 1990, covered property confiscated between 1955 and 1961, but in early 1991 the Federal Assembly decided to extend this back to 1948. About 70,000 properties are now in the process of being restored to their original owners. This issue has delayed the passage of the law on privatization of large enterprises. The draft law, still under consideration as of March 1991, is also more eclectic than originally envisaged: the enthusiasm of the Minister of Finance for the voucher method of privatization has been tempered by political pressures and expert economic advice, and the draft also envisages the use of direct sales. Between 40 and 80 per cent of an enterprise's shares, according to various criteria, can be disposed of in exchange for vouchers. But implementation of the scheme will await the conversion of state enterprises to joint-stock companies, which will not begin before spring 1991. The Law on Small Privatization, covering about 100,000 shops, restaurants and small businesses, was passed in October 1990. These were offered directly for sale to Czechoslovak citizens at auctions, the first of which – in January 1991 – were judged to have been very successful.[16]

'Strong government'?

Despite the differences in their economic starting-points, the most obvious of which is the rather more favourable position of Czechoslovakia in terms of its internal economic balance and external indebtedness in comparison with Poland and Hungary, the basic tasks confronting the new governments are similar, and they face many common political challenges. All three countries have introduced stabilization programmes to tackle budget deficits and bring about long-delayed structural adjustments. Price liberalization and the introduction of internal convertibility of the currency have been introduced with the aim of opening up the economies to the world market and generating real prices that should force enterprises to use resources more efficiently. Demonopolization of the industrial structure, measures to stimulate competition and the formation of new private firms, and the reorganization or liquidation of chronically unprofitable enterprises are in preparation or beginning to be implemented. The collapse of the CMEA, the transition to hard-currency trade with former socialist trading partners, the crisis in the Soviet economy, and the economic fall-out of the Gulf war have all generated enormous pressures for acceleration of the transition, while at the same time intensifying the problems involved and the social counter-pressures.

The political challenges confronting the new governments come from the as yet only partially dismantled structure of corporatist interests and from popular expectations shaped by past experience. While there may be a general acceptance of the need for structural adjustment, there is an equally widespread expectation that such transformation should not be allowed to encroach on the interests of any major social group. As one Polish commentator observed, 'For a considerable part of the society the understanding and accepting of the rules of market economy finishes at the level of expectations of quick success and reaching a Western standard of consumption.'[17] The problem is, of course, that these expectations are unrealistic, and the fears of the significant sections of the workforce of unemployment and the rising cost of living are wholly justified. These have only been reinforced by observation of the impact of 'shock' tactics on East Germany since economic unification in July 1990. The new East-Central European governments have as yet only rudimentary social security nets in place, and are unable to finance them adequately without external aid, which must be a priority in Western aid packages.

The governments must seek to mobilize political support from new economic groups with an interest in change, who expect to benefit from the transition to a market economy. In the short term, such groups (especially new businessmen) are limited in numbers, scattered and politically fragmented, while the organized interests of traditional state industries are still highly influential. Because privatization is only at a most preliminary stage, the bulk of the economy is, and will continue to be for some years to come, state-owned, as a result of which governments find it extremely difficult to avoid being drawn back into patterns of corporatist interaction with major economic interest groups, particularly in threatened traditional industries. Moreover, there are strong expectations on the part of the population that the new 'democratic' governments will be even more responsive to all their various demands than the former communist regimes. Thus the pattern of making direct demands on the government as 'employer', as if it had both the resources and the responsibility to respond, remains far stronger than the pattern of active searching by individuals and enterprises for ways of adapting to and seizing new opportunities offered by new economic conditions. Moreover, where change in the pattern of interest articulation is taking place, this seems only to complicate the government's task: pluralization has brought competition between new unions and interest-based parties to win support by making ever sharper attacks on the government and ever higher demands on the state's overstretched resources. Where governments give in to demands in order to avert social revolt, they merely delay the necessary changes, confirm popular expectations, and provoke further demands from other aggrieved groups.

The country studies that follow do not pretend to give a comprehensive survey of the progress of transition in each case; rather, they focus on the ability of the governments to sustain their internal cohesion, parliamentary support and popular credibility as they take the first steps.

Poland

The Mazowiecki government, installed with the approval of the Sejm on the 12 September 1989, was based on a compromise reached after two weeks of hard bargaining between Solidarity leaders and the official parties (the PUWP, UPP and DP). Solidarity nominated the Prime Minister and one of the Deputy Prime Ministers. It also took control of six ministries (the key economic posts of Finance and Industry, as well as Housing, Labour Affairs, Education and Culture), and five ministers without portfolio (chief of the Prime Minister's Office, Chairman of the Economic Council, Chairman of the Planning Office, rural development, and relations with political parties). The PUWP, UPP and DP were each given a Deputy Prime Ministerial post, held in combination with a specific ministry. The UPP took the Agriculture, Justice, Health and Environment Ministries; the DP took Internal Trade, Technology and Communications; and the PUWP secured control of Internal Affairs, Defence, Transport and Foreign Trade. The independent Krzysztof Skubiszewski took the Foreign Affairs portfolio. A further element of the compromise 'deal' was the continuation of Jaruzelski as President of the Republic.

This government won the support of the Sejm, voting 402 to nil in favour, with 13 abstentions. But from the outset it was 'a disparate government of dissidents, *apparatchiks*, Catholics, liberals, positivists and professionals; people from different political and social backgrounds, with different kinds of qualifications and experiences'.[18] Moreover, despite the extent of parliamentary support, many Solidarity deputies were unhappy with the compromise. For example, Rural Solidarity had been disappointed in not being given the Agriculture portfolio, but the UPP had insisted on this as a condition of its participation in the coalition. Instead, however, Rural Solidarity accepted the post of Minister without Portfolio in charge of rural development. A more fundamental problem for many deputies was the extent of communist participation. The presence in the government of General Kiszczak, Jaruzelski's right-hand man in the imposition of martial law, as Minister for Internal Affairs was hard to swallow, and the extent of general dissatisfaction with the compromise within the Citizens' Parliamentary Caucus was signalled by the refusal of large numbers to vote in favour of Jaruzelski's continued tenure of the Presidency.[19] It was not so much the internal heterogeneity of the government as the continued presence of representatives of the old order that was to prove the weak point in the government's authority, eventually leading to its demise.

From the start, however, the government, especially Mazowiecki in person, enjoyed a high level of popular support, as evidenced by opinion polls during its early months. Mazowiecki's support fluctuated between 93 per cent and 85 per cent in polls conducted between November 1989 and March 1990.[20] The political changes appeared at first to have provided the essential popular basis for dealing decisively with the collapsing economy. But the government and Solidarity were well aware that this support could not be taken for granted: the population was impatient for real improvement in the economy, and promises of democracy alone were unlikely to sustain their allegiance. Moreover, Mazowiecki's unwillingness to further destabilize the administrative machinery of government by wholesale purges of the *nomenklatura* ran the risk of discrediting the new regime by making the political change appear merely musical chairs at the top, while the old faces remained to confront the population directly at lower levels.

The new government sought to bolster its legitimacy by presenting its economic programme both frankly and honestly, but also by emphasizing that changes would be made only on the basis of extensive consultation and negotiation with all interested parties. Mazowiecki adopted the terminology of the 'social market economy', thereby trying to reassure people that welfare considerations would not be swept aside.[21] At the same time, Finance Minister Leszek Balcerowicz called for 'courage, solidarity and willingness to sacrifice' on the part of the population, stressing the need for consistency and radicalism in economic policy – a 'surgical incision' – in the interests of everyone. He also appealed for support in *moral* terms with deep popular resonance, promising 'an economy in which skill, knowledge, talent, able hands and the willingness to work are what counts. We have to break away from the false game in which people pretend to work and the state pretends to pay. The alternative we are proposing is a life of success instead of a life of pretence.'[22]

Public support for the Balcerowicz programme reached its height, 35 per cent, in January 1990 at the point of its implementation, but it was unevenly distributed among different social groups. Younger people up to age 24, those with higher education, Solidarity trade-union members, and those assessing their personal economic situation as 'average' or 'good' showed around 45 per cent support or higher, while in other groups, around 25 per cent or less supported it.[23] But as the programme began to make its effects felt, this already far-from-solid social backing rapidly began to erode. By April, social support for the programme had fallen to a mere 9 per cent, and open social unrest had become an imminent threat. Although the stabilization had had considerable success in bringing monthly inflation down from 78.6 per cent at the end of 1990 to 4.7 per cent, it had done this at the cost of a deep recession, which cut industrial output and real wages by over 30 per cent in the first quarter. The gains won by the cut in inflation – for example, the reappearance of food in the shops – were not offset in the public's mind by the losses in real wages. Thus the government's claims that the strategy was working overall in the right direction cut little ice with the public.

It was against this background that the strains emerged within Solidarity between competing conceptions of its role, as described in the preceding chapter. The movement's leaders, especially those in government and parliament but also many of its regional trade-union organizers and political activists, continued to see it as a 'social movement', centred on the task of bringing about systemic change; Solidarity union activists, on the other hand, facing stiff competition in the enterprises from the surviving former 'official' trade-union movement, OPZZ, were far more convinced of its role as direct defender of workers' interests. Strikes, for example among railway workers in May 1990, saw Solidarity's rank-and-file pitted against the Solidarity government. The bedrock of Solidarity's strength remained in the large, monopolistic enterprises, whose workers were severely affected by the reduction of subsidies, and by the impact of recession and the strict anti-inflationary wage controls imposed by the Balcerowicz plan. In the summer, farmers began a series of protests, culminating in a road blockade, in support of their demands for guaranteed minimum purchase prices and preferential credits, which heightened conflict between the various groups competing for rural support – Rural Solidarity, the UPP and the other claimants to the prestigious mantle of the interwar Peasants Party. This eventually led to the withdrawal of the UPP (by now renamed the Polish Peasants' Party) from the government coalition.[24]

It was in these conditions of rising popular militancy that Walesa was able to step forward as mediator between government and society. His success in intervening to bring strikes to an end served to demonstrate the need to incorporate him into a formal position of power, from which he could contribute his considerable personal authority and political skills to the task of transition from within the government, rather than against it. The obvious post for him was the Presidency, but to get him there would require the immediate abandonment of the Round Table Agreement, which had guaranteed Jaruzelski's tenure, and a further election. It thus involved opening up political conflict within Solidarity while the economic transition was in mid stream, which the Mazowiecki team wanted at all costs to avoid but which it eventually was forced to accept.

The main problem of the Presidential election campaign from an economic point of view was the lack of real alternatives to the Balcerowicz plan. In order to justify his challenge to Mazowiecki, Walesa had to some extent to exaggerate his criticism of the methods by which the plan was being implemented, promising a more radical, accelerated approach while at the same time seeming to suggest that the social costs, particularly unemployment, could be mitigated. One of his advisers even suggested the repudiation of Poland's foreign debt and the lifting of wage controls, so-called 'corrections' that were condemned by Balcerowicz as fundamentally undermining the whole programme and its achievements to date.[25] On the campaign trail, Walesa was also heard to reaffirm his commitment to the basic goals of the Balcerowicz plan and his respect for Balcerowicz personally, but sought to generate popular understanding of the need for every individual to play an active part in the process. However, the crowds that turned out to cheer him proved far more responsive to his attacks on the government, the *nomenklatura* and, on occasion more or less explicitly, the Jews than to his exhortations for greater self-reliance, to which they gave a chilly reception.[26] Walesa was driven further towards cheap rhetoric by the emergence of unexpectedly strong popular enthusiasm for an outsider, Stanislaw Tyminski, an émigré businessman who went far beyond what Walesa and his more responsible supporters could promise by way of a quick and painless path to prosperity. His success in beating Mazowiecki into third place in the first round of the elections was a profound shock to Solidarity leaders in both factions, and forced Mazowiecki's supporters to back Walesa for the second round, which secured his election.

Thus Walesa took over as the first freely elected President of Poland, and a further step towards democracy was made. But the political costs have been high, and it is not yet clear that the benefits will prove sufficient to offset them. Walesa's personal prestige was damaged by his failure to win outright in the first round, which required over 50 per cent of the vote. He won 40 per cent to Tyminski's 23 per cent and Mazowiecki's 20 per cent. Moreover, in some of the regions particularly hard-hit by the transition economic policies, such as the coal-mining centre in Katowice region, Tyminski even won more votes than Walesa, indicating the erosion of confidence in Walesa among precisely those people he had sought to incorporate. Tyminski's support even rose slightly in the second round, to 26 per cent (although the absolute number of his votes dropped slightly), demonstrating an alarming degree of resilience in the face of a barrage of criticism and ridicule aimed at him by the combined forces of Solidarity. Walesa won just under 75 per cent of the votes cast; but, at 53.4 per cent, turnout was relatively low. Moreover, when Walesa was finally able to put together a new government under the economist Krzysztof Bielecki, the continuity in economic policy, and dependence on the former economic team of the Mazowiecki government, were clear. Balcerowicz was reappointed Finance Minister, and altogether eight of the nineteen ministries stayed in the same hands as before. One might well ask whether it had all been worthwhile: indeed, for many of Mazowiecki's supporters, satisfaction at the evidence of continuity was mingled with deep irritation at such 'final proof that Walesa's presidential campaign [had been] a transparent grasp for power';[27] while many of Walesa's campaign supporters were equally dissatisfied with it precisely because of the degree of continuity it embodied. The public is unlikely to be any more impressed, having abstained in large numbers, voted for the demagogue Tyminski, or been won over to Walesa by vague promises of concessions and social protection that he will now be hard put to deliver.

Hungary

On the face of it, the outcome of the spring 1990 general election in Hungary provided far more promising conditions for the formation of an effective government than was the case in Poland, in that it represented a clean break with the past and enjoyed full democratic legitimacy. The swing of voters in the second round of the election gave the HDF a convincing lead, but not a majority of seats in the National Assembly. They won 165 of the 386 contested seats (a further eight seats were reserved for ethnic minority representatives). But there was the basis for a promising coalition with the Independent Smallholders' Party (ISP) and the Christian Democratic People's Party (CDPP), which won 44 and 21 seats respectively. There was a considerable degree of compatibility in the basic political orientation of these parties, and negotiations began between them. But the formation of the coalition was not rapid – the new Prime Minister, Antall, finally presented his team for parliamentary approval on 23 May. It won the support of 218 deputies, with 126 voting against and 18 abstentions.[28]

The HDF naturally dominated the coalition, taking eight of the fifteen ministries (Foreign Affairs, Defence, Internal Affairs, Trade and Industry, Education and Culture, Justice, Transport and Communications, and Environment), in addition to the post of Prime Minister occupied by Antall. The ISP took the Agriculture and Labour Ministries, and the

CDPP took the Ministry of Public Welfare. Two non-party experts were given the key economic posts at the Ministries of Finance and International Economic Relations. Several major weaknesses in the team were apparent from the start. First of all, the ISP, which had insisted on taking the agricultural portfolio, had a highly controversial policy of returning all agricultural land to its 1947 owners, which had been the centre-piece of its electoral programme, and on which it was to prove quite inflexible. Many people, not only in the opposition parties but within the HDF itself, had great misgivings about the practical feasibility of this policy, and certainly were not willing to give it the high priority which it held for the ISP. Moreover, the ISP leadership itself was rather deeply divided on the question of the coalition in the first place. Some provincial ISP activists had in the past developed much stronger personal connections with leading figures in the Free Democrats, and favoured coalition with them rather than with the HDF. This was not politically realistic, but it did produce an open challenge to the leadership at the ISP's national conference following the elections, calling into doubt the party's ability to deliver support to the government.

The high risks of drawing the ISP into government led many political commentators to advocate instead the formation of a 'grand coalition' between the two major parties, the HDF and the AFD; but Antall had firmly ruled this out at the time of the second round of the elections, and by this time relations between leading personalities in the two parties had degenerated as a result of the fierce, often personalized polemics of the election campaign. It was indeed unlikely that a more satisfactory working relationship in government could have emerged with the AFD than with the ISP. However, a promising degree of cooperation between the two major parties appeared early on in the life of the first parliament, when the HDF secured the AFD's agreement to modify the two-thirds majority requirement for the passage of major pieces of legislation by parliament. In return, the HDF supported the resolution of the hitherto contentious issue of the Presidency along the lines preferred by the AFD: namely, that the Presidency should play a figurehead role and be indirectly elected by the National Assembly. Moreover, the HDF backed an AFD candidate for the post, the widely respected writer Arpad Goncz. Thus an important constitutional issue, which was to bedevil Polish politics, was laid to rest,[29] and the stage seemed set for a rather mature, cooperative relationship between government and opposition in parliament.

The HDF itself was far from wholly united. Antall's centrism, which had been so vital in broadening the party's electoral appeal, was not to the taste of the more radical populist intellectuals who had founded the movement back in 1987. These people were held at arm's length by Antall in forming his government, but they had taken up important positions in the party's press and publicity machines, from which vantage point they threatened to fire off critical salvoes at the leadership. In June 1990, the HDF leadership met to attempt to resolve these tensions, and also to avert a threatened breakaway from the HDF by some provincial party groups that were unhappy with the complexion of the government.[30]

A further weakness of the HDF was the absence of a sizeable cohort of economic experts within its ranks from which to draw to fill the key economic posts, and to provide the intellectual back-up necessary for rapid drafting of an economic programme. The problem was that the vast majority of the best-known economic experts had either joined, or were strongly in sympathy with, the AFD. This, as one prominent Hungarian commentator put it, 'ensured that the government would have to put up with a large amount of back-seat driving' from the leading opposition party in parliament.[31] This is indeed how it turned out in the government's first months: 'Government and opposition parties often reversed roles, the opposition putting forward its own draft bills and the government, in turn, attacking them rather than defending its own agenda.'[32]

Crucial factors in the HDF's election victory had been Antall's successful self-projection as a level-headed statesman capable of surmounting petty party politicking, and above all his promise of gradualism as opposed to Polish-style 'shock therapy' in the economy. He freely compared his role with that of Churchill, Adenauer and Kennedy in interviews with the Western press.[33] The Hungarian character, he explained, would not respond well to the challenge of radical economic policies on account of the pessimistic, depressive national psychology and high propensity to suicide: 'Many Hungarians throw life away out of bitterness. To promise blood, sweat and tears is not going to give strength to the Hungarians as it did to the British.'[34] Antall's approach was thus not to leap into action in the economy, but to ask parliament for a period of '100 days' grace', in order to give the government time to draw up a well-considered programme on the basis of thorough analysis of the facts. But at the end of this period of apparent inaction, the government was exposed to a barrage of critical assessments from all sides: instead of the promised stability, a crisis of legitimacy was emerging.[35]

The basic problem was identified by the sociologist Ivan Szelenyi in the weakness of genuine popular support for the government as a result of the low turnout (46 per cent) in the second round of the general election. It was thus a government based on a 'majority of a minority',[36] which rested on the votes of only about a quarter of the electorate. Popular political engagement declined even further between April and the September local government elections, in the first round of which only 33 per cent of town dwellers participated (even in Budapest, only 37 per cent went to the polls), thus falling below the 40 per cent required for a valid election. Participation declined further in the second round.[37] Moreover, the local elections revealed a marked swing away from the parties of the governing coalition in favour of the opposition AFD and Fidesz. The government, Szelenyi claimed, held the 'world record for loss of popularity'. Already at the end of June, less than half those polled by the Hungarian Institute for Public Opinion Research had believed that the government knew how to lead the country out of its economic crisis.

The reasons for this loss of confidence can be found in the failure of Antall's government to combine its gradualism and caution with a sense of purpose and political momentum. People perceived the '100 days' grace' as a period of drift and delay of vital economic policy measures. In particular, no anti-inflationary policy had emerged, but instead a set of price rises had been brought in that merely served to fuel inflation. Containing the budget deficit, the key condition for IMF support for the new government's programme, proved beyond its capacity. As the economic situation deteriorated, gradualism increasingly appeared to be a luxury that the country could not afford; caution lost its attractiveness to a population now anxious for decisive action. The government was seeking, but failing to come up with, a convincing and distinctive alternative programme to that presented by its political rivals. Instead, its approach seemed reactive and *ad hoc*. 'What in fact is the economic policy of the government?' asked Laszlo Lengyel in August:

> It would be an oversimplification to say that it has chosen the way of caution as opposed to shock therapy. What are the proposals of the Ministry of Finance (admittedly details not known) for a complete overhaul of the system of prices, wages and taxation with a view to making the currency convertible if not shock therapy? What too about the switch to hard-currency trade with the Soviet Union and other Comecon countries? The problem is, however, that the non-coordinated implementation of these policies risks providing the shock without the therapy.[38]

The government's long-awaited 'Economic Programme for National Renewal' was published in September 1990. Despite its 220 pages, it met with outspoken criticism for vagueness.[39] Even at the time of publication, it was clear that the government would be unable to meet the legislative programme it had set itself for 1990, which was already far behind schedule.[40] Confusion and disorganization within the government, inefficiency in drafting legislation and managing the parliamentary timetable, and poor coordination of the work of committees and plenary sessions were blamed for this.[41] Moreover, the open political conflict within the government over agricultural reprivatization had held up the drafting of a coherent policy on ownership as a whole, and had weakened the government's general credibility. The ISP, one commentator found, had behaved like a 'wild opposition party', not a responsible partner in power, and this reflected badly on Antall's political judgment in bringing the ISP into the coalition in the first place.[42] The style of politics at the top had also alienated the public: the work of the National Assembly had rapidly descended from its initial promise of providing constructive debate to being dominated by 'personalized, ideologized, narrowly party-political and shrill-voiced debates', resurrecting some of the worst features of prewar parliamentary tradition.[43] As one HSP deputy put it, people still saw politics as 'the mischief-making of gentlemen' while all the time their living standards were deteriorating.[44] Opinion polls revealed that only 40 per cent of the population had confidence in the National Assembly.[45] The sense of a looming political crisis thus gathered strength as the country entered what promised to be a difficult autumn.

The crisis came with the government's decision on 25 October to introduce overnight a 66 per cent rise in the price of gasoline. It justified this by the 30 per cent shortfall in oil deliveries from the Soviet Union, which was facing the country with severe shortages, and by the need to bring domestic prices in line with world prices, which had risen sharply following the Iraqi invasion of Kuwait. Taxi drivers in Budapest immediately responded by a strike, and were soon joined by private freight carriers. They blockaded the capital city's main arterial roads, and similar actions spread throughout the provinces, bringing the country to a standstill within a day. The government's response to this was heavy-handed and inflexible. Antall had gone into hospital the day before, having returned ill and exhausted from a visit to the USA, leaving the conduct of affairs in the hands of the Minister of the Interior, Balazs Horvath, who was to prove personally inept in handling the conflict. The official reaction was to rule out compromise on economic grounds, and to brand the action as the work of a small minority of reckless law-breakers. Horvath ordered the police to move in to break up the road-blocks; but this order was later withdrawn, apparently after the Budapest police themselves, painfully aware of their very low public reputation, refused to use force against the protestors. A complete breakdown in authority was averted by the intervention of President Goncz, who calmed the situation by announcing that, as commander-in-chief of the armed forces, he was not prepared to call on the military to impose order; instead, he appealed to the government to suspend the price increases and begin negotiations with the strikers for a solution, and asked parliament to convene in emergency session.

Negotiations (covered live on television) began on 26 October, under the aegis of the National Interest Coordinating Council, a new mediating body representing employers, private entrepreneurs, workers, trade unions and farmers' associations.[46] The striking drivers called in the National Association of Trade Unions (the reformed former official trade unions), and the League of Democratic Trade Unions also participated. A key role was played by Janos Palotas, Chairman of the National Council of Private Entrepreneurs, who rapidly won widespread popular respect for his articulate presentation of the drivers' case: he argued that the essence of the grievance was not the price rises *per se*, the need for which was understood by the drivers; it was the rate of increase, which in 1990 had in fact been much faster than the rate of increase in the world price. The drivers were aggrieved that the government was using the gasoline price increases as an easy means of raising additional revenue in their desperation to stem the rising budget deficit, which they had been unable to control. It was thus in effect a hidden tax increase, an 'easy option' for the government and one that thrust the burden of transition unfairly onto a particular group. Finally, the government was forced to concede this point, and negotiations concluded with a reduced rate of price increase, and agreement not to impose further taxes on gasoline.

In the process of televised negotiations, the really precarious state of the economy, and of the energy situation in particular, was fully exposed to the public. The acute difficulties facing the government became clear, but its political standing was badly impaired at the same time. A popularity index, devised by the Institute for Public Opinion Research, revealed immediately after the crisis that Antall's rating stood at zero, while his chief economic ministers scored strongly negative ratings.[47] But if the government's authority was battered, the opposition parties, and the National Assembly itself, fared little better, having been relegated to the sidelines throughout the crisis. Their strongly worded denunciations of the government's ineptitude were already well-worked refrains, and they proved unable to step forward with a positive solution. President Goncz emerged as the only incumbent of an official state position with a favourable popular image. Thus the formal political institutions had failed, while the new interest-representing organizations had demonstrated a remarkable political efficacy: in them, not in the parties or the government, the 'silent majority' of urban-dwelling non-voters had begun to recognize a channel for the expression of their interests.

In these circumstances, in which both the government and the opposition face the challenge of rebuilding the credibility of their parties and overcoming the lack of legitimacy of the whole political system, the case for a 'grand coalition' between the HDF and the AFD became stronger in the view of many Hungarian political commentators.

More recently, in March 1991, Fidesz took the initiative in proposing a new Round Table of all the parliamentary parties, in order to hammer out a basic consensus on fundamental issues of political and economic transformation, including privatization, and to secure the smoother, more business-like passage of urgently needed legislation. This new 6-party Round Table was still under discussion in April when this book went to press. To what extent can this be expected to improve the situation? On the one hand, it might serve to temper the attacks of the opposition on government, and draw a wider range of economic experts into policy formation. Round Table consultation could strengthen the government's claim that policies are based on consideration of the 'national interest', and the demonstrated efforts of the politicians to work together more constructively might help restore the credibility of the new political institutions with a population alienated by the spectacle of government paralysis and divisive party politics in parliament. However, it might also be seen as a setback for the development of pluralistic politics, which depends on fostering public acceptance of competition and diversity as healthy, normal features of a democracy. The problem, as perceived in Hungary today, is that the level and forms of conflict and competition are ineffective and counterproductive in the current extraordinary conditions, and, to this extent, the establishment of a special extra- parliamentary forum may be justified. But the longer-term implications of this early admission of the failure of parliament to fulfil its proper function should be noted: *ad hoc* political innovations, such as this latest Round Table, have a tendency to develop a life of their own and to become entrenched features of the political system. This is by no means to suggest that Hungary is departing from the democratic path, but rather that its demo-cracy seems likely to evolve along the neo-corporatist lines characteristic of its closest neighbour, Austria, rather than along the more pluralistic line of, for example, Britain or the United States.

Czechoslovakia

The 'Government of National Unity' approved by the Czechoslovak Federal Assembly on 10 December 1989 had been formed under the direct pressure of mass demonstrations in the streets of Prague and the threat of a general strike by the majority of the industrial labour force. It was essentially a temporary government, to last only six months until the free elections of June 1990. Its 'legitimacy' was circumscribed by its extraordinary legal status; but, on the other hand, it derived a sort of revolutionary legitimacy from the circumstances of its birth in the euphoric 'velvet revolution'. Great hopes were vested in it by the people, and there were high expectations of the rapid implementation of radical reforms, including in the economy.

A central feature of the Government of National Understanding was the remarkably substantial part initially played in it by members of the communist party, including the Federal Prime Minister, Marian Calfa, two of the six Deputy Prime Ministers (who were also the Czech and Slovak Republican Prime Ministers) and five other ministers. A further two, First Deputy Prime Minister Valtr Komarek and Deputy Prime Minister Vladimir Dlouhy, were party members at the time of their appointment, but distinguished themselves in their contributions to the 'velvet revolution' in November and were in fact nominees of the Civic Forum (CF). The apparent strength of communists reflected not so much CPCS bargaining power in the negotiations as the self-consciously conciliatory stance of the CF leadership under Vaclav Havel. Indeed, it would have been hard to find sufficient suitable personnel otherwise, given the particularly high level of party membership among middle-aged, professionally qualified males in Czechoslovakia. All the communists in the government depended on the approval of the CF and Public Against Violence (PAV). They were selected on the basis of their personal competence and relatively clean records. The vast majority of them quickly resigned from the CPCS, and some of them rather soon resigned their government posts to make way for new non-communist appointees. Thus CPCS membership did not become a major point of division in the new government, which worked rather effectively as a team of independent experts.

However, divisions did appear over the crucial questions of the scope and pace of economic transformation. All the key economic posts were occupied by former colleagues from the Institute of Prognostics (long-term forecasting), directed by Valtr Komarek, which had been the main source of reformist thinking in the 1980s. Komarek, a reform communist who had been involved in the 1968 economic reforms, advocated a slower pace of marketization, placing the emphasis on achieving structural reforms (demonopolization and phased closure of non-viable enterprises) in the economy before liberalizing prices and foreign trade. He also appeared to be much more cautious on the question of privatization. Vladimir Dlouhy and the new Minister of Finance, Vaclav Klaus, by contrast, argued for a more radical and rapid transition to a marketized economy.

The differences of opinion rested in part on divergent assessments of the stability and underlying strength of the Czechoslovak economy. The absence of serious internal disequilibrium (monetary overhang and shortages) and large foreign debts, which posed intractable problems in Poland and Hungary, seemed to suggest the possibility of a less traumatic, more gradual economic transition. But Dlouhy and Klaus were less convinced that these undoubted advantages could be enough to avert the shock that any substantial progress towards marketization entailed. They argued for shock therapy even in the Czechoslovak context, seeing gradualism as a recipe for prolonging the period of dislocation and obstructing the progress of marketization. But there were deeper political differences between the respective positions: Komarek espoused more clearly social democratic positions, while Klaus presented himself as a Friedmanite advocate of neo-liberal economics.

This division within the government became open in the spring of 1990, and appeared particularly clearly in the election campaign.[48] Although the government secured the passage of a significant package of economic legislation in April 1990, the division within its ranks slowed down the implementation of radical change in the economy, and led to some poorly coordinated actions. For example, the 18.6 per cent devaluation of the Czechoslovak crown that Klaus put into effect immediately after taking office in January generated a controversial surge in purchases by Western tourists, and his strongly restrictive amendments to the 1990 budget were criticized for stifling fledgling private enterprise.

In this dispute, the ambiguous legitimacy of the Government of National Understanding played a key part. Komarek bolstered his argument for gradualism by pointing to the transitional and non-elected nature of the government, which, he felt, limited its right to take decisions on really fundamental, systemic issues. Klaus, on the other hand, could refer to the 'revolutionary legitimacy' of the government: public opinion polls showed that the people were ready, even impatient, for radical change in the economic field and expected the government to act without delay.[49] Clearly, resolution of the problem had to wait for the formation of the new government after the elections.

The convincing win by the CF and PAV in the elections gave them a majority of seats (170 of a total 300) in the Federal Assembly. However, the new government remained a coalition, excluding communists but drawing in two representatives of the Slovak Christian Democratic Movement and six independents, who joined the five CF and two PAV members. Marian Calfa, who by now had joined PAV, remained Prime Minister. In the formation of the government, two major concerns affected the distribution and allocation of posts. First, the new economic team signalled a shift in favour of the radical approach to economic transformation. Komarek left the government, to be replaced as Deputy Prime Minister with overall responsibility for the economy by the independent economic expert Vaclav Vales. Dlouhy was reappointed as Minister for the Economy, and Klaus retained his post at Finance, both CF nominees. Reports circulated that President Havel had tried to shift Klaus to the chairmanship of the State Bank, suggesting a significant difference of opinion between the Presidency and the government on economic matters, to which we will return below.

The second, increasingly salient, concern was to ensure a satisfactory balance of Czechs and Slovaks in the government. A major factor in Calfa's reappointment was undoubtedly his Slovak origins, which counterbalanced the Czech Havel, re-elected as President by the new Federal Assembly. Ten members of the new government were Czechs and six were Slovaks.[50] It was thus the product of a delicate balancing act between considerations of political affiliation, ethnic origin, and professional competence and experience. The coalition not only aimed to satisfy the need for broad political support, thus averting charges made by the communists (with more than a hint of cynicism) of a 'new monopoly of power' on the part of the CF/PAV, but also had to pay heed to rising Slovak assertiveness. In any case, the CF/PAV position in the Federal Assembly was not unassailable, owing to the complexity of that body as

97

a bicameral (or more accurately, semi-tricameral) assembly comprising a House of the People, with proportional representation from the Czech and Slovak Republics (with 101 and 49 seats respectively), and a House of Nations, with two equal 75-member sections for Czechs and Slovaks. In order to pass major constitutional changes, a three-fifths majority is required in each of the three bodies – the House of the People and the two national sections of the House of Nations – voting separately. Other legislation requires a simple majority in each of the bodies, and a vote of no-confidence is possible by a simple majority in any one of them. Although the CF/PAV enjoyed a majority of 87 seats in the House of the People, and the CF had a majority of 50 seats in the Czech section of the House of Nations, PAV won only 33 of the 75 Slovak section seats. Moreover, the heterogeneous and undisciplined nature of the two movements argued for securing as broad a range of political support for the government as was compatible with its overall coherence.

Although the new government, sworn in on 29 June, had the basis for consensus among its leading economic ministers on the goal of economic transformation and on the need for speed in its implementation, there was still room for some discussion on the means, particularly of privatization, as explained in the first part of this chapter. Consensus was reached by the end of summer 1990 on a 'Scenario for Economic Reform', setting out the main tasks ahead and a timetable for implementing the necessary legislation.[51] This was discussed and approved by the Federal Assembly in September.[52] But the main obstacle to rapid progress in the economic field came from elsewhere – from the rapidly escalating constitutional crisis posed by Slovak nationalism.

The Slovak National Party had won nine seats in the House of Nations, and public opinion polls in the summer of 1990 showed a rising trend of popular support for it in Slovakia. More important still was the balance of forces in the newly elected Slovak National Council, the representative assembly of the Slovak Republic. An early warning of the potential of the nationality issue to divert attention away from economic issues had been given in March and April, when an unexpectedly bitter controversy broke out in the Federal Assembly over the renaming of the state. Slovak deputies were not satisfied with simply removing the word 'socialist' from the title of the state and renaming it the Czechoslovak Federal Republic; they demanded as well, and succeeded in obtaining, the abandonment of the word 'Czechoslovak' in favour of 'Czech and Slovak'. The existence of a 'Czechoslovak' identity was rejected as an artificial construct, implicitly 'centralist' in its connotations.

After the elections, it became clear that the federal issue had to take precedence over everything else, and particularly over economic transformation, since the division of economic powers and resources were at the heart of both issues. As long as the federal government's economic team argued for the necessity of a unified economic policy and strategy for systemic transformation without the consent of the Slovaks, the political legitimacy of the programme would be undermined. A major source of grievance on the part of both Czechs and Slovaks was the cross-subsidization of the two republics by central redistribution of resources. Radical decentralization of the republican budgets was thus necessary. But, given the divergent economic conditions in the two republics, there was also room for suspicion on the part of the federal government that decentralized control over resources and over general economic policy-making might lead to divergent paths in the implementation of the economic transformation programme. Slovakia is burdened with a rather high proportion of economically vulnerable industrial enterprises. Preferential investment in Slovakia under the Husak regime in the 1970s (a source of Czech resentment at the time) had been directed into heavy industry, defence production and oil-refining industries, which cannot be sustained under open market conditions.

The political dilemma is thus that economic decentralization to the republics will allow the Slovak government to intervene to a far greater extent than the federal government wishes, thus slowing down or diverting the course of economic transformation and fracturing the unity of the economy; whereas centralism, in the interests of a coordinated transition, threatens to undermine the legitimacy not only of the economic transformation but also of the federal government and the state itself, should Slovaks become persuaded that the burdens of the economic transformation are falling disproportionately on their shoulders. Economic transformation could easily be presented as something 'done to' Slovaks by Prague as a form of punitive reprisal for their awkward assertiveness.

The resolution of this issue clearly could not wait until the formulation of the new Federal and Republican Constitutions, which were expected to take up most of the two-year term of the newly elected legislatures. Instead, in August 1990 a series of intricate negotiations between the federal and republican governments was begun, with a view to reaching agreement on an extensive amendment to the existing 1968 federal constitution. In this, the Slovak government, a coalition comprising thirteen PAV members, seven CDM members and three Slovak

Democratic Party members, played the role of chief antagonist against the federal government, with the Czech government acting sometimes as ally with the Slovaks against the federal government, but more often as intermediary between them. The PAV Prime Minister of Slovakia, Vladimir Meciar, proved to be a difficult negotiating partner, as PAV itself shifted to a more assertively autonomist position in consequence of the gathering momentum of events in Slovakia and under pressure from its CDM partners. Both PAV and the CDM sought to bolster their own popular legitimacy by appropriating some of the nationalist rhetoric that was proving very effective for the Slovak Nationalist Party – but at the cost of allowing nationalist rhetoric to dominate the language of political debate, and, in PAV's case, provoking the first signs of a rift within the movement. In the meanwhile, the CF's 'shift to the right' under its new chairman Vaclav Klaus, was viewed with misgivings by the Slovaks as heralding a trend towards centralism in the Czech movement, further straining relations within the Federal government.

Eventually, by 12 December, a formulation of the amendment was adopted with the assent of all three legislatures, averting, for the time being, a constitutional crisis. The provisions were thus able to come into effect on 1 January 1991, alongside the first major steps in economic transformation: price liberalization, internal convertibility and small-scale privatization. The federal government retains control over defence, foreign affairs, foreign trade, the central bank, federal taxation, customs and price reforms. The federation is to raise its own revenue directly in both republics, rather than relying on transfers from them. Several major ministries, including industry and trade, have been abolished at the federal level and transferred to the republics. The republics are to enjoy jurisdiction over those areas not specifically reserved for the federation. But several areas remained undecided in the negotiations, and have been left to the general redrafting of the new constitutions. These include control over transport and the state-run media. Control over the oil pipeline was transferred to a Czech-Slovak joint-stock company. Ownership of assets remains in the hands of the republic in which they originated, but this does not include ownership of natural resources, which awaits later agreement. The federal government retains the right to control the distribution of energy resources in emergency conditions. A particularly contentious issue still to be confronted is whether the federal government alone, or each of the two republics, should have the right to declare a state of emergency.[53] All the indications are that this state of affairs is at best a temporary expedient; at worst, the unsatisfactory compromises and incompleteness of the agreement could give rise to further misunderstanding, mistrust and mutual recrimination.

In the course of the first year of post-communist politics in Czecho-slovakia, the role of the Presidency has been vital, and has grown beyond what its occupant, Vaclav Havel, envisaged on his re-election in June.[54] His reappointment of the little-known Calfa as Prime Minister ensured he would have no personal rival as national figurehead, and he is still regarded by the majority of the population as the guarantor of the achievements of the 'velvet revolution'. Thus, from the start, he accepted a weighty share of the burden of sustaining the authority of the state in the transition period; but this share grew rapidly in the course of the autumn's difficult power-sharing negotiations, in which he took part at crucial junctures (and which to some significant extent dented his personal popularity among Slovaks). Finally, alarmed at the prospect that the Federal Assembly would fail to agree to the laborious constitutional amendment, he appealed to it to consider granting temporary additional powers to the rather ill-defined Presidential office, to allow the President to intervene in the case of governmental deadlock, which had at times threatened to arise in the power-sharing talks. In the end, this did not prove necessary in order to secure the passage of the amendment. His other suggestions – for the introduction of a Constitutional Court and national referendums – which were also designed to provide interim institutional mechanisms for breaking deadlocks, remain to be decided by the Assembly.

In the meanwhile, the Presidential Office has grown in order to meet Havel's need for expert advice, which is hardly surprising given the responsibilities he has accumulated. To some commentators, this has appeared as an unwelcome development, overshadowing the authority of the government. Indeed, in the economic field, some signs of tension between the 'Castle' (the Presidential Office) and the government have emerged. There is a distinct difference of emphasis on the 'social' and the 'market' aspects of the 'social market economy' between the President and his economic adviser, Richard Wagner, on the one hand, and the more overtly neo-liberal Finance Minister, Vaclav Klaus on the other. Klaus's election to the chairmanship of the CF represented a definite blow to Havel's prestige, since he clearly backed another candidate. Although personal relations between these two men, the leading figures in Czech politics, appear to be strained, the extent of the real divergence of their views on fundamental issues should not be overstated. Havel has accepted the need for a radical approach in the economy, and if Klaus is to sustain political support for his programme of economic transformation (and also if he wants to further his undoubtedly high political ambitions), he too will have to find a way to accommodate moderate demands for consideration of the social welfare issues involved. Above all, he will need to avoid falling into the trap of claiming the programme of economic transformation as the sole property of the right wing of the political spectrum, to which he personally is committed.

Popular acceptance and legitimation of the programme of economic transformation can be won only if it is presented as necessary in the general, national interest and as the common objective of all major political groupings, and of Czechs and Slovaks alike. The two parts of the CF seem now to have found a framework for cooperation on the road to economic transformation; they have yet to find equally committed Slovak partners to join them on the way.

CONCLUSION

No one ever pretended the process of political and economic transformation in East Central Europe would be easy or painless, but it has been rendered even more difficult in the first year of post-communism by the rapid deterioration of the external environment, which has always had such a powerful influence over the internal development of these small, politically and economically vulnerable countries. The collapse of the CMEA in 1990 and the immediate transition to convertible-currency trade at the start of 1991, the disappearance of the important East German market with that country's absorption into a united Germany, and, above all, the political and economic crisis in the Soviet Union, still by far the most important trading partner for East Central Europe – all these processes have immensely complicated the tasks of economic transformation. Western aid has become more urgently needed than ever to support the transformation of these countries, but just at a time when the Western capacity and will to meet the need seems to show signs of faltering: major Western economies are facing slowdown or recession; Germany, always a key partner for East-Central European countries, has become – it is to be hoped temporarily – introverted and self-absorbed in the task of unification; and the crisis in the Gulf in 1990 and 1991 has drawn off not only Western economic resources but, even more importantly, Western political attention and energy. And yet it is clear to all those who continue to follow developments in East Central Europe that adequate economic support for the political and economic transformation of these countries is in the West's direct strategic interest as well as its moral responsibility.

As the difficulties facing East Central Europe have piled up, doubts

have surfaced here and there about the likelihood of a successful outcome of the process of transformation. The inexperience of the politicians, the naiveté of popular expectations, the weakness of democratic
political culture and the re-emergence of intransigent nationalists are all
cited as reasons for expecting the task of economic transformation to run
aground or be diverted back into variants of protectionism and statism.
Certainly the possibility of failure cannot be discounted, but it is surely
too early for conclusive judgments on this account. As yet, the evidence
does not seem to me sufficient to persuade me to abandon my own
conviction that Poland, Hungary and Czechoslovakia will continue to
develop politically along democratic paths and economically towards
open market systems. This conviction ultimately rests on my understanding of the underlying motive force of these countries' development
since the Second World War, culminating in 1989: the steady maturation
of the popular will to 'rejoin the West', to live under democratic government and to work in a free economy.

NOTES

Chapter 1

1 See the very useful collection of essays edited by M. McCauley, *Communist Power in Europe 1944-49* (London: Macmillan, 1977).

2 See for definitions P. Schmitter, 'Still the Century of Corporatism?' in P. Schmitter and G. Lehmbruch (eds.), *Trends towards Corporatist Intermediation* (Beverly Hills and London: Sage Publications, 1979); and, applied to the Soviet Union, V. Bunce, 'The Political Economy of the Brezhnev Era: the Rise and Fall of Corporatism', *British Journal of Political Science,* vol. 13, April 1983.

3 H. G. Skilling, 'Group Conflict and Political Change' in Ch. Johnson (ed.), *Change in Communist Systems* (Stanford, CA: Stanford University Press, 1970).

4 The classic account of this development in the Soviet context, which is equally applicable to the East European cases, is by R. V. Daniels, 'Soviet Politics since Khrushchev' in J. Strong (ed.), *The Soviet Union under Brezhnev and Kosygin* (New York: Van Nostrand, 1971).

5 Compare with the optimistic view of Hungarian political evolution in W. T. Robinson, *The Pattern of Reform in Hungary* (New York, Washington and London: Praeger, 1973).

6 See J. Batt, *Economic Reform and Political Change in Eastern Europe* (London: Macmillan, 1988).

7 G. Blazyca, 'The Degeneration of Central Planning in Poland' in J. Woodall (ed.), *Policy and Politics in Contemporary Poland* (London: Pinter, 1982); K. Poznanski, 'Economic Adjustment and Political Forces: Poland since 1970' in E. Comisso and L. Tyson (eds.), *Power, Purpose and Collective Choice: Economic Strategy in Socialist States* (Ithaca and London: Cornell University Press, 1986); 'The Political Limits to Economic Reform in Hungary 1968-78', in *Economic Reform.*

8 'Economic Adjustment and Political Forces'.
9 *Economic Reform.* See also A. Pravda and B. Ruble (eds.), *Trade Unions in Communist States* (London: Allen and Unwin, 1986).
10 See I. Berend, *A Magyar Gazdasagi Reform Utja* (Budapest: Kozgazdasagi es Jogi Konyvkiado, 1988), pp. 370ff.
11 See Z. Gitelman, 'Is Hungary the Future of Poland?' *East European Politics and Societies*, vol. 1, no. 1, winter 1987.
12 See Chapter 5.2, 'Economic Reform in Poland', in Economic Commission for Europe, *Economic Survey of Europe in 1989/90* (New York: United Nations, 1990).
13 J. Brada, 'Is Hungary the Future of Poland, or is Poland the Future of Hungary?', *East European Politics and Societies*, vol. 2, no. 3, fall 1988, p. 468.
14 E. Kerpel and D. Young, *Hungary to 1993: Risks and Rewards of Reform*, Special Report no. 1153 (London: Economist Intelligence Unit, November 1988), p 106.
15 A stimulating but ultimately inconclusive discussion of the concept of 'leadership drift' and its applicability to different communist regimes can be found in a special issue of *Studies in Comparative Communism*, vol. XXII, no. 1, spring 1989.
16 See G. Kolankiewicz, 'Poland and the Politics of Permissible Pluralism', *East European Politics and Societies*, vol. 2, no. 1, winter 1980.
17 See R. Tokes, 'Hungarian Reform Imperatives', *Problems of Communism*, vol. XXXIII, no. 5, September-October 1984.
18 See G. Schöpflin, R. Tokes and I. Volgyes, 'Leadership Change and Crisis in Hungary', *Problems of Communism*, vol. XXVII, no. 5, September-October 1988.
19 'Economic Adjustment and Political Forces', p. 287.
20 A detailed account of the composition of the political elite under Kadar is to be found in R. Tokes, 'Hungary's New Political Elites: Adaptation and Change 1989-90', *Problems of Communism*, vol. XXXIX, no. 6, November-December 1990.
21 See 'A Social Contract: Conditions for Political Renewal', translated from the *samizdat* periodical *Beszelo* in *East European Reporter*, vol. 3, no. 1, 1987, pp. 54-8.
22 A translated version is available: see L. Antal, et al., 'A Debate on "Change and Reform"', *Acta Oeconomica*, vol. 38, nos 3-4, 1987.
23 See P. Lewis, 'The Long Good-Bye: Party Rule and Political Change in Poland since Martial Law', *Journal of Communist Studies*, vol. 6, no. 1, March 1990, pp. 32-3.
24 P. Lewis, *Political Authority and Party Secretaries in Poland* (Cambridge: Cambridge University Press, 1989), p. 299.
25 See 'Poland and the Politics of Permissible Pluralism'.

26 See M. Csanadi, 'Beyond the Image: the Case of Hungary', *Social Research*, vol. 57, no. 2, summer 1990.

27 See 'The Long Good-Bye', p. 36.

28 See J. Pataki and K. Okolicsanyi, 'Government Changes - Too Little, Too Late?', *Radio Free Europe Hungarian Situation Report*, no. 6, item 3, 9 May 1989.

29 M. Markus, 'Overt and Covert Modes of Legitimation in East European societies' in T. Rigby and F. Feher (eds.), *Political Legitimation in Communist States* (London: Macmillan, 1982).

30 The term is elaborated fully by E. Hankiss, 'Demobilization, Self-Mobilization and Quasi-Mobilization in Hungary, 1948-1987', *East European Politics and Societies*, vol. 3, no. 1, winter 1989.

31 See 'Towards a New Democratic Compromise', p. 26.

32 See the account by Solidarity's historian, Jerzy Holzer, 'Seven Years after August', *East European Reporter*, vol. 3, no. 1, 1987, p. 4.

33 See A. Brumberg, 'Poland: the New Opposition', *New York Review of Books*, 18 February 1988, pp. 23-7.

34 'A New Social Contract: Conditions for a Political Renewal', from *Beszelo*, special issue, June 1987, translated in *East European Reporter*, vol. 3, no. 1, 1987, p. 55.

35 This aspect of the crisis is emphasised by Schöpflin et al., in 'Leadership Change and Crisis in Hungary'; and G. Kolankiewicz and P. Lewis, *Poland: Politics, Economics and Society* (London: Pinter, 1988), Chapter 2; The sociologist Elemer Hankiss spoke of the 'escape into illness', a passive and self-destructive response on the part of society to the regime's strategy of social control by 'demobilization'. See 'Demobilization, Self-Mobilization and Quasi-Mobilization', pp. 124-5.

36 See I. Gabor, 'The Second (secondary) Economy', *Acta Oeconomica*, vol. 22, no. 3-4, 1979.

37 See interview with Elemer Hankiss, 'First Society, Second Society', *East European Reporter*, vol. 3, no. 1, winter 1989, p. 63.

38 On the 1956 events, see F. Fejto, *A History of the People's Democracies* (Harmondsworth: Pelican, 1974), and Z. Brzezinski, *The Soviet Bloc* (Cambridge MA: Harvard University Press, 1967).

39 Husak to the XIV Congress of the CPCS: see *XIV. sjezd KSC* (Prague: Svoboda, 1971), p. 153.

40 M. Hruskovic, 'Towards the further development of Economic Science', *Czechoslovak Economic Papers*, no. 13, 1972, p. 17.

41 See V. Kusin, *From Dubcek to Charter 77* (Edinburgh: Q Press, 1978), pp. 69-89.

42 I developed these points more fully in 'Czechoslovakia under Gorbachev', paper presented to the conference on Gorbachev's Eastern Europe, Radio Free Europe, Munich, June 1988. Official statistics themselves betray the

extent to which the purges affected the quality of enterprise management: the proportion of enterprise managers and administrative workers with the requisite level of education and qualifications for their posts declined between 1966 and 1972, particularly in the Czech Lands, according to data in *Statisticka Rocenka CSSR* (Prague: SNTL, various years).

43 See 'Analyza vyvoje ekonomicke teorie v Ceskoslovensku v sedesatych letech', special issue of *Politicka Ekonomie*, no. 9, 1972.

44 See the CPCS Central Committee document, *Lessons of the Crisis Development in the Party and Society after the XIII Congress* (Prague: Svoboda, 1970).

45 The 'Set of Measures' was in fact so hedged about by qualifications and compromises that it did not have any perceptible impact anyway on the performance of the economy. See F. Levcik, 'Czechoslovakia: Economic Performance in the Post-Reform Period and Prospects for the 1980s' in US Congress Joint Economic Committee, *East European Economic Assessment* (Washington DC: USGPO, 1981), esp. pp. 420-24.

46 Strougal made an important speech advocating reform on 27 January 1987, published just two days after Gorbachev's momentous speech to the CPSU Central Committee on political reform. Translated excerpts from Strougal's speech are available in BBC *Summary of World Broadcasts*, EE/8478 B, 29 January 1987, pp. 2-8.

47 H. G. Skilling reminds us of the contribution of bureaucratic traditions in Czech political culture in explaining Stalinism in Czechoslovakia. See 'Stalinism and Czechoslovak Political Culture' in R. C. Tucker (ed.), *Stalinism: Essays in Historical Interpretation* (New York: Norton, 1977).

48 See K. Dyba, 'Adjustment to International Disturbances: Czechoslovakia and Hungary', *Acta Oeconomica*, vol. 34, no. 3-4, 1985.

49 See the comparison of Hungary and Czechoslovakia by K. Dyba, 'Dve desetileti dvou ekonomik', *Hospodarske Noviny*, no. 29, 1988, pp. 10-11.

50 See, for example, the essay by the Czechoslovak Chartist Petr Pithart, 'Social and Economic Developments in Czechoslovakia in the 1980s', parts I and II, *East European Reporter*, vol. 4, nos 1 and 2, winter 1989/90 and spring/summer 1990.

51 The concept was elaborated by T. H. Rigby with respect to the Brezhnev regime in the early 1970s: see 'The Soviet Leadership: Towards a Self-Stabilising Oligarchy?', *Soviet Studies*, vol. XXII, no. 2, October 1970.

Chapter 2

1 This paraphrase of Brezhnev's argument was memorized by the Czechoslovak communist Z. Mlynar, who was present at the Moscow meeting at which Brezhnev spoke. See Mlynar, *Nightfrost in Prague* (London: C. Hurst, 1980), p. 240.

2 See K. Dawisha, 'The 1968 Invasion of Czechoslovakia: Causes, Consequences and Lessons for the Future', and P. Summerscale, 'The Continuing Validity of the Brezhnev Doctrine' in K. Dawisha and P. Hanson, *Soviet-East European Dilemmas* (London: Heinemann/RIIA, 1981).

3 K. Dawisha, *Eastern Europe, Gorbachev and Reform* (Cambridge: Cambridge University Press, 1990), second edition, p. 198.

4 See G. Schöpflin, 'The Brezhnev Doctrine after Twenty Years', *Radio Liberty Report on the USSR*, vol. 1, no. 4, 27 January 1989.

5 The most important speeches in which Gorbachev addressed East European questions were in Prague on 10 April 1987, (see 'For a "Common European Home", for a New Way of Thinking' published in pamphlet form by Novosti Press Agency, Moscow); and in Yugoslavia in March 1988 (see 'Speech at Yugoslavia's Federal Assembly', *Moscow News*, 23 March 1988).

6 See *Eastern Europe, Gorbachev and Reform*, pp. 198-201; and A. Rahr, '"New Thinking" takes hold in the Foreign Policy Establishment', *Radio Liberty Report on the USSR*, vol. 1, no. 1, 6 January 1989.

7 For example, E. Shevardnadze and A. Yakovlev at the February 1990 CPSU Central Committee plenum. See BBC *Summary of World Broadcasts*, SU/ 0684 C/19, 9 February 1990.

8 As referred to in '"New Thinking" takes hold'.

9 See *Pravda*, 8 February 1990, translated in BBC *Summary of World Broadcasts*, SU/0684 C/19, 9 February 1990.

10 See Dawisha and Valdez, 'Socialist Internationalism in Eastern Europe', *Problems of Communism*, vol. 36, no. 2, March-April 1987; and, by the same authors, 'The New Internationalism in Eastern Europe' in R. Laird (ed.), *Soviet Foreign Policy: Proceedings of the Academy of Political Science*, vol. 36, no. 4, 1987.

11 J. Valdez, 'Crises, Contradictions and Eastern Europe: Soviet Theoretical Debates and Reform 1982-86', paper presented to the IV World Congress of Soviet and East European Studies, Harrogate, England, 21-26 July 1990.

12 See *Eastern Europe, Gorbachev and Reform*, pp. 198-201.

13 This became apparent with the publication of a report on the proceedings of a major conference at the Ministry of Foreign Affairs in July 1988. See 'The 19th All-Union CPSU Conference: Foreign Policy and Diplomacy', *International Affairs*, no. 10, 1988.

14 See for example the very interesting document on Eastern Europe prepared by a group of scholars from the Moscow Institute of the Economics of the World Socialist System, for a conference in the United States: 'East-West Relations and Eastern Europe (A Soviet-American Dialogue)', *Problems of Communism*, vol. 37, no. 3-4, May-August 1988.

15 Including, to some extent, Dawisha herself: see the much more cautious

conclusions in the first (1988) edition of *Eastern Europe, Gorbachev and Reform.*

16 See T. Kuhn, *The Structure of Scientific Revolutions* (Chicago: University of Chicago Press, 1970), second edition.

17 R. Asmus, 'Evolution of Soviet-East European Relations under Mikhail Gorbachev', *Radio Free Europe Background Report* RAD/153 (Eastern Europe), 22 August 1989, p. 8.

18 This was the argument of G. Schöpflin, in 'The Brezhnev Doctrine after Twenty Years'. See also C. Gati, *The Bloc that Failed* (Bloomington and Indianapolis: Indiana University Press/CSIS, 1990).

19 See 'Evolution of Soviet-East European Relations', p. 18.

20 'Negotiating (and Renegotiating) Pacts' in O'Donnell and Schmitter (eds.), *Transitions from Authoritarian Rule*, part IV 'Tentative Conclusions about Uncertain Democracies' (Baltimore and London: Johns Hopkins University Press, 1986), p. 38.

21 Even the apparently 'liberal' HSWP leadership still thought in these terms, as revealed by a leaked Politburo resolution which referred to the opposition as 'enemy groups'. See 'Under the Political Counter', *East European Reporter*, vol. 2, no. 3, 1987.

22 These concepts are derived from L. Bruszt, '1989: the Negotiated Revolution in Hungary', *Social Research*, vol. 57, no. 2, summer 1990.

23 See A. Michnik, 'The New Evolutionism', reproduced in *Letters from Prison and Other Essays* (Berkeley, Los Angeles and London: University of California Press, 1985).

24 A discussion of these issues is provided by T. Judt, 'The Dilemmas of Dissidence: the Politics of Opposition in East-Central Europe', *East European Politics and Societies*, vol. 2, no. 2, spring 1988, especially pp. 225-31.

25 See 'Towards a New Democratic Compromise: Interview with Adam Michnik', *East European Reporter*, vol. 3, no. 2, March 1988.

26 'The First Steps towards Democracy: an Interview with Adam Michnik', *East European Reporter*, vol. 3, no. 4, spring/summer 1989, p. 37.

27 See A. Brumberg, 'Poland: the New Opposition', *New York Review of Books*, 18 February 1988.

28 *Transitions from Authoritarian Rule*, p. 38.

29 See 'Towards a New Democratic Compromise', pp. 27-8.

30 A sample of this approach is M. Siedlecki, 'Time for Positive Action', *East European Reporter*, vol. 3, no. 4, spring/summer 1989, p. 35.

31 Quoted in Z. Barany and L. Vinton, 'Breakthrough to Democracy: Elections in Poland and Hungary', *Studies in Comparative Communism*, vol. 23, no. 2, summer 1990, p. 193.

32 A peculiarity of the electoral system was that in order to register a vote, electors had to *delete* all the names on the ballot except that of the chosen

candidate. Thus 'negative voting' on the scale that occurred in the Polish elections required quite a lot of positive effort. See 'Breakthrough to Democracy'.

33 For a more detailed account of the Polish elections, see P. Lewis, 'Non-Competitive Elections and Regime Change: Poland 1989', *Parliamentary Affairs*, vol. 43, no. 1, January 1990.

34 An account of the electoral law is given in J. Batt, 'The Hungarian General Election', *Representation*, summer 1990.

35 On interwar Hungarian politics, see A. Janos, *The Politics of Backwardness in Hungary 1825-1945* (Princeton NJ: Princeton University Press, 1982).

36 On political development in Hungary in general since 1987, see J. Batt, 'Political reform in Hungary', *Parliamentary Affairs*, October 1990.

37 On the electoral system and the results in detail, see 'The Hungarian General Election'.

38 See the report of the commission of enquiry set up by the Federal Parliament to investigate the origins of and the responsibility for the events of 17 November 1989, reproduced in translation in BBC *Summary of World Broadcasts*, EE/0763 B/3-4. Also J. Obrman, 'November 17, 1989 – Attempted Coup or the Start of a Popular Upheaval?', *Radio Free Europe Report on Eastern Europe*, vol. 1, no. 27, 6 July 1990.

39 See P. Martin, 'The New Czechoslovak "Government of National Understanding"' and 'Biographies of Members of the Federal Government', *Radio Free Europe Report on Eastern Europe*, vol. 1, no. 2, 12 January 1990.

40 See J. Batt, 'After Czechoslovakia's Velvet Poll', *The World Today*, vol. 46, nos 8-9, August-September 1990.

Chapter 3

1 A useful discussion of the concept of 'political culture' can be found in the introduction to A. Brown and J. Gray (eds.), *Political Culture and Political Change in Communist States* (London: Macmillan, 1979), second edition.

2 See M. Marody 'Perceptions of Politics in Polish Society', *Social Research*, vol. 57, no. 2, summer 1990.

3 The term is used by G. Breslauer to describe the Brezhnev period in Soviet politics, but is highly appropriate for East European communist regimes as well. See 'On the Adaptability of Soviet Welfare-State Authoritarianism', in K. Ryavec (ed.), *Soviet Society and the Communist Party* (Amherst: University of Massachusetts Press, 1978).

4 See L. Bruszt '"Without us but for Us?": Political Orientation in Hungary in the Period of Late Paternalism', *Social Research*, vol. 55, nos 1-2, spring/summer 1988.

5 Outstanding accounts of the interwar political history of these countries are provided by J. Rothschild, *East Central Europe between the Two World Wars* (Seattle and London: University of Washington Press, 1974) and A. Janos, *The Politics of Backwardness in Hungary 1825-1945* (Princeton NJ: Princeton University Press, 1982).

6 On the origins of these attitudes in the interwar period, see G. Ionescu, 'Eastern Europe' in E. Gellner (ed.), *Populism* (London: Weidenfeld and Nicolson, 1969).

7 On this pattern of political economy in Hungary, see Chapter 7 of *Economic Reform and Political Change in Eastern Europe*.

8 See I. Szelenyi, *Soviet Entrepreneurs* (Madison: University of Wisconsin Press, 1988) and A. Aslund, *Private Enterprise in Eastern Europe* (London: Macmillan, 1985).

9 See I. Deak, 'Uncovering Eastern Europe's Dark History', *Orbis*, vol. 34, no. 1, winter 1990.

10 M. Keens-Soper, 'The Liberal State and Nationalism in Postwar Europe', *History of European Ideas*, vol. 10, no. 6, 1989, p. 694.

11 A useful survey of the situation as of February 1990 is provided by Radio Free Europe research paper 'Political Parties in Eastern Europe', dated 10 February 1990.

12 See T. Garton-Ash, *The Polish Revolution: Solidarity* (London: Jonathon Cape, 1983).

13 See A. Touraine, et al., *Solidarity* (Cambridge: Cambridge University Press, 1983), p. 99.

14 Z. Pelczynski, 'Solidarity and the "Rebirth of Civil Society"' in J. Keane (ed.), *Civil Society and the State* (London: Verso, 1988), pp. 371-2.

15 This comparison has been explored by D. Mason in 'Solidarity as a New Social Movement', *Political Science Quarterly,* vol. 104, no. 1, 1989.

16 See 'Solidarity and the "Rebirth of Civil Society"'.

17 L. Vinton and Z. Barany, 'Breakthrough to Democracy: Elections in Poland and Hungary', *Studies in Comparative Communism*, vol. XXIII, no. 2, summer 1990, p. 197.

18 Ibid., p. 197.

19 See A. Sabbat-Swidlicka, 'Walesa moves to "Tidy Up" Citizens' Committee Movement', *Radio Free Europe Report on Eastern Europe*, vol. 1, no. 25, 22 June 1990; and A. Sabbat-Swidlicka, 'The Future of the Citizens' Committee Movement', *Radio Free Europe Report on Eastern Europe*, vol. 1, no. 27, 6 July 1990.

20 See L. Vinton, 'Walesa prevails in Citizens' Committee Conflict', *Radio Free Europe Report on Eastern Europe*, vol. 1, no. 30, 27 July 1990.

21 See L. Vinton, 'Solidarity's Rival Offspring: Center Alliance and Democratic Action', *Radio Free Europe Report on Eastern Europe*, vol. 1, no. 38, 21 September 1990.

22 For a vivid partisan portrayal of the contrasting identities of the two factions by a leading member of ROAD, see A. Michnik, 'The Two Faces of Europe', *New York Review of Books*, 19 July 1990.

23 See J. Pehe, 'Civic Forum and Public Against Violence Strive to Become More Effective', *Radio Free Europe Report on Eastern Europe*, vol. 1, no. 42, 19 October 1990.

24 On Masaryk's legacy, see J. Trojan, 'Democracy and its spiritual foundations', *East European Reporter*, vol. 4, no. 3, autumn/winter 1990.

25 'Obcanske forum a volby 1990', Civic Forum leaflet, Prague, 1990.

26 L. Blazek 'Perspektivy poslani Obcanskeho fora', *Forum*, vol. 1, no. 8, 21 March 1990, p. 3.

27 See J. Pehe 'The Civic Forum before the Election Campaign Begins', *Radio Free Europe Report on Eastern Europe*, vol. 1, no. 14, 6 April 1990.

28 See interviews with Petr Miller, Martin Palous and Ivan Gabal in *The Economist*, 20 January 1990, p. 60.

29 The then head of the Civic Forum, Petr Pithart, spoke out against these dangers on Czechoslovak television in January 1990: see BBC *Summary of World Broadcasts*, EE/0668 B/1-2, 22 January 1990.

30 See J. Pehe 'The Controversy over Communist Managers', *Radio Free Europe Report on Eastern Europe*, vol. 1, no. 36, 7 September 1990.

31 J. Kavan, et al., 'OF na rozcesti?', *Forum*, vol. 1, no. 12, 18 April 1990, p. 1.

32 See P. Janyska, 'Jak dal OF?', *Respekt*, vol. 1, no. 34, 31 October-6 November 1990, p. 2.

33 In May 1988, the HSWP Central Committee expelled four intellectuals from the party for having joined the HDF.

34 See E. Oltay 'Imre Pozsgay resigns from the Hungarian Socialist Party', *Radio Free Europe Report on Eastern Europe*, vol. 1, no. 48, 30 November 1990.

35 See J. de Weydenthal 'Communists Dissolve Party, Set Up a New Social Democratic Group', *Radio Free Europe Report on Eastern Europe*, vol. 1, no. 7, 16 February 1990.

36 See J. Pehe 'Changes in the Communist Party', *Radio Free Europe Report on Eastern Europe*, vol. 1, no. 48, 30 November 1990.

37 For a useful study of the Slovak National Party, see Z. Butorova and T. Rosova, 'Slovenska narodna strana: myty, ritu, vyznavaci', *Respekt*, no. 38, 28 November-4 December 1990, p. 4.

38 See A. Sabbat-Swidlicka, 'Peasant Party Politics', *Radio Free Europe Report on Eastern Europe*, vol. 1, no. 5, 2 February 1990.

Chapter 4

1 R. Dahrendorf, *Reflections on the Revolution in Europe* (London: Chatto and Windus, 1990), p. 85.

2 *Reflections on the Revolution*, p. 92.

3 The classic elaboration of this model was that of the Polish economist Wlodzimierz Brus: see his *Economics and Politics of Socialism* (London: Routledge and Kegan Paul, 1972) and *Socialist Ownership and Political Systems* (London: Routledge and Kegan Paul, 1976).

4 See L. Antal, 'Development - With Some Digression', *Acta Oeconomica*, vol. XXIII, nos 3-4, 1979.

5 J. Kornai, 'The Hungarian Reform Process: Visions, Hopes and Reality', *Journal of Economic Literature*, vol. XXIV, December 1986.

6 T. Bauer, 'The Hungarian Alternative to Soviet-Type Planning', *Journal of Comparative Economics*, vol. 7, 1983, pp. 304-16.

7 See, for an unfashionably sceptical view, M. Nuti, 'Privatization of Socialist Economies: General Issues and the Polish Case', paper presented to the OECD Conference on the Transformation of Planned Economies, Paris, 20-22 June 1990.

8 A very useful paper clarifying the issues is B. Milanovic, 'Privatization in Post-Communist Societies', mimeo, Washington DC, World Bank, 12 September 1990. I have also relied heavily on Janos Kornai, *The Road to a Free Economy* (New York and London: W. W. Norton, 1990).

9 *The Road to a Free Economy*, p. 90.

10 Ibid., p. 91.

11 Ibid., p. 54.

12 Ibid., p. 82.

13 See Act VI of 1988 on Business Organization, reproduced in T. Sarkozy (ed.), *Foreign Investments in Hungary: Law and Practice* (Budapest: Lang Kiado, 1989).

14 See M. Jackson, 'The Privatization Scorecard for Eastern Europe', *Radio Free Europe Report on Eastern Europe*, vol. 1, no. 50, 14 December 1990; also N. Denton, 'Privatization Programme under Pressure', survey of Hungary in *The Financial Times*, 17 September 1990.

15 See I. Grosfeld and P. Hare, 'Privatization in Hungary, Poland and Czechoslovakia', *European Economy*, forthcoming 1991.

16 For a more detailed account of Czechoslovak developments, see P. Martin, 'Privatization: a Balance Sheet', *Radio Free Europe Report on Eastern Europe*, vol. 2, no. 5, 1 February 1991.

17 J. Hausner, 'The New Interests Structure', in *Polish Economy in Transition* (Warsaw and Cracow: Zycie Gospodarcze, 1991), p. 41.

18 'Mazowiecki's New Government Line Up', *Radio Free Europe Situation Report Poland/14*, 12 September 1989, p. 4.

19 See P. Lewis, 'Non-Competitive Elections and Regime Change: Poland 1989', *Parliamentary Affairs*, vol. 43, no. 1, January 1990, p. 102.

20 A. Rychard, 'Limits to the Economic Changes in Post-Communist Poland: Sociological Analysis' in S. Gomulka and C. Lin (eds.), *Limits to Reform*

and Transition in Communist Countries (Oxford: Oxford University Press, forthcoming 1991).

21 L. Vinton, 'Mazowiecki's Political Agenda for 1990', *Radio Free Europe Report on Eastern Europe*, vol. 1, no. 10, 9 March 1990.

22 Quoted in L. Vinton 'Solidarity Forces Pledge Support as the Government Prepares Economic Changes', *Radio Free Europe Report on Eastern Europe*, vol. 1, no. 2, 12 January 1990, p. 21.

23 'Limits to the Economic Changes'.

24 See A. Sabbat-Swidlicka, 'Polish Peasants Party Withdraws Support for Mazowiecki's Government', *Radio Free Europe Report on Eastern Europe*, vol. 1, no. 41, 12 October 1990.

25 See L. Vinton, 'Economic Issues in the Presidential Campaign', *Radio Free Europe Report on Eastern Europe*, vol. 1, no. 48, 30 November 1990.

26 Ibid., p. 14.

27 L. Vinton 'New Prime Minister Outlines Program, Nominates Cabinet', *Radio Free Europe Report on Eastern Europe*, vol. 2, no. 4, 25 January 1991, p. 23.

28 See A. Reisch 'New Government Combines Party Politicians with Professional Experts', *Radio Free Europe Report on Eastern Europe*, vol. 1, no. 25, 22 June 1990.

29 See K. Okolicsany, 'President Arpad Goncz and the Office of the Presidency', *Radio Free Europe Report on Eastern Europe*, vol. 1, no. 42, 19 October 1990.

30 See 'Weekly Record of Events: Hungary', *Radio Free Europe Report on Eastern Europe*, vol. 1, no. 25, 22 June 1990, p. 41.

31 L. Lengyel, 'New Ingredients in the Goulash', *East European Reporter*, vol. 4, no. 3, autumn/winter 1990, p. 37.

32 A. Reisch, 'The New Coalition Government: Its First 100 Days and Beyond', *Radio Free Europe Report on Eastern Europe*, vol. 1, no. 41, 12 October 1990.

33 See for example, N. Denton, 'Profile: Prime Minister Jozsef Antall', survey of Hungary in *The Financial Times*, 17 September 1990, p. 8.

34 Ibid.

35 I. Szelenyi, 'Demokracia, legitimacio es polgari engedetlenseg', *Magyar Hirlap*, 9 November 1990.

36 Ibid.

37 See Appendix.

38 'New Ingredients in the Goulash', p. 37.

39 Translated excerpts from the programme can be found in *East European Reporter*, vol. 4, no. 3, autumn/winter 1990.

40 See K. Okolicsany, 'The Economic Programme for National Renewal', *Radio Free Europe Report on Eastern Europe*, vol. 1, no. 50, 14 December 1990.

41 See 'New Ingredients in the Goulash', and 'The New Coalition

Government: Its First 100 Days'.

42 L. Keri, 'Szaz nap turelmetlenseg', *168 Ora*, vol. 2, no. 34, 28 August 1990.

43 'Demokracia, legitimacio es polgari engedetlenseg'.

44 Zoltan Kiraly, reported in BBC *Summary of World Broadcasts*, EE/0830 [i], 31 July 1990.

45 'Demokracia, legitimacio es polgari engedetlenseg'.

46 See A. Reisch, 'The Gasoline War: Order of Chaos?', *Radio Free Europe Report on Eastern Europe*, vol. 1, no. 45, 9 November 1990.

47 See 'Demokracia, legitimacio es polgari engedetlenseg'.

48 See the reports of two simultaneous press conferences at which Komarek and Klaus presented their rival views, 'Nejde o vitezstvi, ale o nas', *Mlada Fronta*, 9 June 1990, pp. 1 and 2.

49 See 'Strach je spatny radce', *Lidove noviny*, 11 June 1990, p. 6.

50 See P. Martin, 'The New Governments', *Radio Free Europe Report on Eastern Europe*, vol. 1, no. 30, 27 July 1990.

51 See 'Scenar ekonomicke reformy', *Hospodarske noviny*, 4 September 1990, special supplement.

52 See P. Martin, '"Scenario for Economic Reform" Adopted', *Radio Free Europe Report on Eastern Europe*, vol. 1, no. 42, 19 October 1990.

53 See J. Obrman and J. Pehe, 'Difficult Power-Sharing Talks', *Radio Free Europe Report on Eastern Europe*, vol. 1, no. 49, 7 December 1990.

54 For an outline of his proposed reorganization of the Presidential office, see his address to the Federal Assembly, translated in BBC *Summary of World Broadcasts*, EE/0805 [i], 2 July 1990.

APPENDICES

APPENDICES:
ELECTIONS IN
EAST CENTRAL EUROPE

Appendix 1: Poland

GENERAL ELECTION
First round: 4 June 1989
Second round: 18 June 1989

Electoral system

The *Sejm* (lower house) comprises 460 seats, of which 161 were open to free competition, 23 were allocated to officially recognized Catholic associations (PAX, Christian Social Association, Polish Social Catholic Union), and the remaining 276 allocated to the Polish United Workers Party, the United Peasants Party and the Democratic Party.

108 multiple-member constituencies returned between two and five deputies, according to size of population.

The *Senate* (upper house) comprises 100 seats, all of which were open to free competition. 47 of the 49 voivodships (regional administrative divisions) returns two Senators, and Warsaw and Katowice return three.

Candidates standing for the open seats had to present a petition signed by 3,000 supporters in order to qualify for entry, or be nominated by one of the official parties or associations.

Candidates for the pre-allocated Sejm seats were presented by the respective parties and associations. Usually, more than one candidate was presented even for these seats, but 35 of the pre-allocated party seats were reserved for a 'national list' of leading politicians (mostly PUWP Politburo members) who stood unopposed.

Voters were presented with separate ballot papers for each Sejm and Senate seat (between four and eight sheets, according to constituency). They marked

119

their choice by deleting all names except that of the chosen candidate on each ballot paper.

In order to be elected on the first round, candidates had to win over 50 per cent of votes cast. If no candidate achieved this, a run-off between the top two candidates took place in the second round.

Results

First round: turnout 62.11%

Sejm – Candidates sponsored by the Citizens' Committees (Solidarity) won 160 of 161 open seats; 1 seat remained undecided; 2 candidates standing unopposed for the 35 'national list' seats were elected, the rest withdrew from the election; 3 candidates standing for the remaining 264 pre-allocated seats were elected, 261 remained undecided.

Senate – Candidates sponsored by the Citizens' Committees won 92 of the seats; the rest remained undecided.

Second round: turnout 25.9%

Sejm – Open seats: 161 won by candidates sponsored by Citizens' Committees. Reserved Seats: 173 Polish United Workers Party; 76 United Peasants Party; 27 Democratic Party; 10 PAX; 8 Christian Social Association; 5 Polish Social Catholic Union.

Senate – The remaining 8 undecided Senate seats were all won by candidates sponsored by Citizens' Committees, except for one, which was won by an independent businessman.

See: P. Lewis 'Non-Competitive Election and Regime Change: Poland 1989', *Parliamentary Affairs*, vol. 43, no. 1, January 1990; Z. Barany and L. Vinton, 'Breakthrough to Democracy: Elections in Poland and Hungary', *Studies in Comparative Communism*, vol. XXXII, no. 2, summer 1990.

LOCAL ELECTIONS
27 May 1990

Electoral system

All seats were open to free competition. Individual candidates were required to present 15 signatures in support in order to enter the ballot. Parties and organizations presented 150 supporting signatures in order to register a party list. Local constituencies with less than 40,000 residents contested a single seat by simple majority. Larger constituencies had multiple seats contested by party lists; seats were allocated proportionally.

Results: turnout 42.27%

Citizens' Committees – 41.43%
Unaffiliated – 37.92%
Polish Peasant Party – 6.54%
Rural Solidarity – 4.32%
Solidarity trade union – 1.74%
Democratic Party – 1.68%
National minorities – 0.65%
Social Democracy of the Republic of Poland – 0.28%
Confederation for an Independent Poland – 0.10%
Christian-Democratic Labour Party – 0.10%
Christian-National Union – 0.10%
Others – 5.14%

Sources: L. Vinton 'Political Parties and Coalitions in the Local Government Elections', *Radio Free Europe Report on Eastern Europe*, vol. 1, no. 26, 29 June 1990; and A. Sabbat-Swidlicka, 'The Polish Local Election Results', ibid.

PRESIDENTIAL ELECTIONS
First round: 25 November 1990
Second round: 9 December 1990

Results
First round: turnout 60%

Lech Walesa – 39.3%
Stanislaw Tyminski – 23.2%
Tadeusz Mazowiecki – 19.9%
Wlodzimierz Cimoszewicz – 10.3%
Roman Bartoszcze – 6.1%
Leszek Moczulski – 2.4%

No candidate won over 50% of the vote as required for outright election; the top two candidates thus entered a second round.

Second round: turnout 53.4%

Lech Walesa – 74.25% (total 10,622,696 votes)
Stanislaw Tyminski – 25.75% (total 3,683,098 votes)

Sources: *Gazeta Wyborcza*, 26 November 1990; and L. Vinton, 'Walesa elected President', *Radio Free Europe Report on Eastern Europe*, vol. 1, no. 51, 21 December 1990.

Appendix 2: Hungary

GENERAL ELECTION
First round: 25 March 1990
Second round: 8 April 1990

Electoral system

The National Assembly (*Orszaggyules*) has 386 seats, of which 176 are allocated to single-member constituencies, 152 are drawn proportionally from party lists presented in multi-member county constituencies, and 58 are drawn proportionally from national party lists on the basis of 'wasted votes' cast in the single-member and county constituencies.

The elections were contested on the basis of free competition.

In order to stand in a single-member constituency, candidates have to present 750 signatures in support from residents in that constituency. To qualify to present a party list in a county constituency, a party/movement has to (a) be legally registered; and (b) be presenting party candidates in one quarter (minimum 2) of the single-member constituencies in the given county.

For the election to be valid in any constituency, a turnout of more than 50% must be achieved. If this is not achieved, a repeat ballot must be held in the second round, which is valid with a 25% turnout.

To gain the seat in a single-member constituency, a candidate must win over 50% of valid votes cast. If no candidate achieves this, the second ballot is contested by those candidates who won over 15% in the first round, or the first three candidates. The candidate with the most votes then takes the seat.

In order to be allocated seats in a county constituency, the party list must win at least 4% of the votes cast nationwide. Seats are then allocated proportionally to the candidates on the party lists in the order determined by the parties. The number of seats per county constituency varies according to size.

Wasted votes (those not yet used to win seats in single-member constituencies or county party lists) are used to allocate seats proportionally to national party list candidates.

See: J. Batt, 'The Hungarian General Election', *Representation*, summer 1990.

Results
First round: turnout 63.2%
Second round: turnout 45.9%

Share of votes for county party lists

	Votes	%
Hungarian Democratic Forum (HDF)	1,214,359	24.7
Alliance of Free Democrats (AFD)	1,050,799	21.4
Independent Smallholders' Party (ISP)	576,315	11.7
Hungarian Socialist Party (HSP)	535,064	10.9
Federation of Young Democrats (Fidesz)	439,649	8.9
Christian Democratic Peoples' Party (CDPP)	317,278	6.5
Hungarian Socialist Workers' Party (HSWP)	180,964	3.7
Hungarian Social Democratic Party (HSDP)	174,434	3.5
Agrarian Alliance	154,004	3.1
Entrepreneurs' Party	92,689	1.9
Patriotic Electoral Coalition	91,922	1.9
Hungarian Peoples' Party	37,047	0.8
Hungarian Green Party	17,951	0.4
6 other parties (under 10,000 votes each)	28,766	0.6

Source: *Magyar Nemzet*, 30 March 1990.
Note: Parties in italics passed the 4% barrier and were allocated regional and national seats.

Final distribution of seats in the National Assembly

Party	Individual seats	Regional seats	National seats	Total seats
HDF	115	40	10	165
AFD	34	34	23	91
ISP	11	16	17	44
HSP	1	14	18	33
Fidesz	1	8	12	21
CDPP	3	8	10	21
Agrarian Alliance	1	0	0	1
Independent	6	0	0	6
Joint Deputy*	4	0	0	4
Total seats filled				386

Source: *Szabadon Valsztott: Parlamenti Almanach 1990* (Budapest: Idegenforgalmi Propaganda es Kiado Vallalat, 1990).
*Deputies representing more than one party (2 joint Fidesz/AFD, one joint Fidesz/AFD/CDPP, one joint Agrarian candidate).

LOCAL ELECTIONS
First round: 30 September 1990
Second round: 14 October 1990

Electoral system

In communities and villages with less than 10,000 inhabitants, mayors and members of the local self-government bodies are elected directly in multi-member local wards. Voters may select as many names from the list on the ballot as there are seats available in the ward. In larger communities (over 10,000), i.e. towns and cities, half the members of the self-government bodies are elected in individual wards, and half from party lists (cf the basic lines of the general election system). The mayors of larger communities are elected indirectly by the members of the self-government body. A turnout of 40% is required for a valid election in a ward.

See: J. Pataki, 'Local Elections Expected to Complete the Political Transition', *Radio Free Europe Report on Eastern Europe*, vol. 1, no. 40, 5 October 1990.

Results

First round: turnout *40.18%* (small communities 50.95; towns and cities 33.09%, among which Budapest 37.39%)
Second round: turnout *28.94%* (small communities 32.2%; towns and cities 27.1%, among which Budapest 32.12%)

Small communities: share of total numbers of mayors and members elected (%)

	Mayors	Members		Mayors	Members
Independents	82.9	71.2	CDPP	1.8	2.8
ISHP	3.7	6.2	Agrarian Alliance	—	1.3
HDF	2.3	4.3	HSP	—	1.1
AFD	1.9	4.0	Others (below 1%)	7.4	9.1

Large communities, towns and cities: share of members elected (%)

	Individual seats	Party list seats
AFD	17.2	20.7
AFD/Fidesz joint	16.9	5.0
Independents	14.9	—
HDF	12.0	18.3
Fidesz	8.4	15.3
ISHP	6.0	7.8
CDPP	5.7	8.0
HSP	2.6	10.1
HDF/CDPP joint	2.5	2.5
HDF/ISHP/CDPP joint	2.4	2.2
HDF/ISHP joint	2.1	—
HSWP	—	1.3
Others (below 1%)	9.3	—

Source: *Magyar Nemzet*, 15 and 16 November 1990.H-pendix 3: Czechoslovakia

Appendix 3: Czechoslovakia

GENERAL ELECTION
8-9 June 1990

Electoral system
The Federal Assembly is bicameral, with 150 seats in the House of the Nations divided into two equal sections of 75 each from the Czech Republic and the Slovak Republic; and 150 seats in the House of the People divided according to the respective population size of the two Republics, 101 seats to the Czech Republic and 49 to the Slovak Republic.

The country is divided into 12 multiple-member constituencies (based on the 10 administrative regions plus Prague and Bratislava). Parties, which must be legally registered, present separate lists of candidates standing for election to the two Houses of the Assembly from the given constituency.

Voters select one party list of candidates for each House. They may also alter the order in which the candidates appear on the list by indicating a special preference for up to four of the names on the party list (if they do not exercise this

125

choice, the order of candidates as they appear on the list is observed). Seats are then allocated in the constituency in proportion to the share of votes cast to each party; but parties have to win more than 5% of the vote in the Czech Republic in order to be allocated seats in any Czech constituency, or 3% of the vote in Slovakia.

Elections were held at the same time for the republican assemblies, the Czech National Council (200 seats) and the Slovak National Council (150 seats), using the same electoral system and constituencies.

See: Law on Elections to the Czechoslovak Federal Assembly (Prague: Orbis, 1990); J. Batt, 'After Czechoslovakia's Velvet Poll', *The World Today*, August/September 1990.

Results

Turnout 96% (Czech Republic 96.79%; Slovak Republic 95.41%)

Share of votes cast (%)

	Czech Rep.	Prague	Slovak Rep.	Bratislava
Civic Forum	53.15	62.47	—	—
Public Against Violence	—	—	32.54	37.12
Christian Democratic Movement	—	—	18.98	14.98
Communist Party	13.48	11.86	13.81	14.28
Slovak National Party	—	—	10.96	16.78
MSD/SMS*	7.89	0.57	—	—
Coexistence	0.08	0.05	8.58	2.18
Christian and Democratic Union	8.69	6.62	—	—
Others below 5% (CR) or 3% (SR)				

Source: *Svobodne slovo*, 12 June 1990.
*Movement for Self-Governing Democracy/Society for Moravia and Silesia (25.20% vote in South Moravia, 15.20% in North Moravia)

Distribution of seats in the Federal Assembly

House of the Nations (150 seats)

Slovak Section (75 seats)
Public Against Violence – 33
Christian Democratic
    Movement – 14
Communist Party – 12
Slovak National Party – 9
Coexistence – 7

Czech Section (75 seats)
Civic Forum – 50
Communist Party – 12
MSD/SMS – 7
Christian and Democratic
    Union – 6

House of the People (150 seats)

Slovak Republic (49 seats)
Public Against Violence – 19
Communist Party – 8
Christian and Democratic
    Movement – 11
Slovak National Party – 6
Coexistence – 5

Czech Republic (101 seats)
Civic Forum – 68
Communist Party – 15
Christian and Democratic
    Union – 9
MSD/SMS – 9

Sources: *Svobodne slovo*, 12 June 1990; *Lidove noviny*, 14 June 1990.

Distribution of seats in the Czech National Council

Civic Forum – 127
Communist Party – 32
MSD/SMS – 22
Christian and Democratic Union – 19
Total number of seats – 200

Distribution of seats in the Slovak National Council

Public Against Violence – 48
Christian Democratic Movement – 31
Slovak National Party – 22
Communist Party – 22
Coexistence – 14
Democratic Party – 7
Green Party – 6
Total number of seats – 150

LOCAL ELECTIONS
23-24 November 1990

Electoral system

A proportional representation system using party lists is also applied to local elections, but with greater provision for independent individuals to stand than in general elections, and no minimum percentage of the vote required in order to win seats.

See: J. Pehe, 'Laws on Local Government Elections Adopted', *Radio Free Europe Report on Eastern Europe*, vol. 1, no. 14, 12 October 1990.

Results

Turnout: Czech Republic 73.55%; Slovak Republic 63.75%

Shares of total votes cast and total local representatives elected in the Czech Republic (%)

	Votes	Seats won
Civic Forum	35.57	31.72
Communist Party	17.24	14.43
People's Party	11.50	12.14
Independents	10.63	27.66
Social Democracy	4.95	1.58
MSD/SMS	4.16	2.56
Socialist Party	3.54	1.58
Greens	3.22	1.34
Agricultural Party	1.52	2.50
Christian Democratic Party	1.27	0.37
Others (44 small parties and movements under 1%)	6.40	4.22

**Shares of total local representatives elected
in the Slovak Republic (%)**

Christian Democratic Movement – 27.4
Public Against Violence – 20.4
Communist Party – 13.6
Independents – 12.8
Coexistence – 6.3
Slovak National Party – 3.2
Farmers' Movement – 3.1
Hungarian Christian-Democratic Movement – 3.0
Democratic Party – 2.3

Sources: *Svobodne slovo*, 26 and 28 November 1990.